Smocking

Traditional & Modern Approaches

Smocking

Traditional & Modern Approaches

Œnone Cave & Jean Hodges

B.T. BATSFORD LTD   LONDON

To Vicky Lugg

© Œnone Cave and Jean Hodges 1984
First published 1984
This paperback edition published 1988

ISBN 0 7134 5879 8

Typeset by Servis Filmsetting Ltd, Manchester
and printed in Great Britain by
Anchor Brendon Ltd
Tiptree, Essex
for the publishers
B.T. Batsford Ltd
4 Fitzhardinge Street
London W1H 0AH

Some of the material in this book was originally
published in *English Folk Embroidery*,
© Œnone Cave 1965, reprinted as *Traditional Smocks
and Smocking*, © Œnone Cave 1979

Cover shows a late nineteenth-century linen smock
decorated with tape lace and cutwork (*Dorset County
Museum, Dorchester*).

Contents

Acknowledgement

The authors would like to extend their grateful thanks to all those people, too numerous to mention by name, whose interest and enthusiasm have helped them during the preparation of this book, and in particular to those who have generously given advice or loaned work for inclusion.

Œnone Cave would like to thank Richard Blount for taking the photographs and Maggie Jordan for her interesting and helpful advice on making up traditional smocks.

Jean Hodges would like to thank all her students, especially those at the Hampton School of Needlework, for their help, support and understanding; Ron Head for the main photography and his cheerful optimism when constantly faced with the near-impossible; Pauline Mackenzie for the fashion and design drawings; Deborah Flint for her valiant work on the word processor; last, and by no means least, her family for their love, constant encouragement and help during periods of despair and occasional moments of elation.

FOR USA READERS

Bias   on the diagonal
Calico   unbleached canvas or muslin
Cords   twisted cords
Cushion   pillow
Cushion pad   pillow form
Iron   press
Piping   welting
Plait   braid
Tacking   basting
Straight grain   straight of grain
Wadding   batting

One

The Evolution of the Smock

During the nineteenth century the smock was a costume widely worn by the English peasantry for labour and leisure alike; it was lavishly ornamented with embroidery, together with the more functional stitchery known to this day as smocking (*1, 2*). The origin of this smock appears more closely related to the *tunica*, originally of Roman origin but still being worn in Saxon times, than to the Anglo-Saxon *smoce* which resembled the chemise and its male equivalent the shirt. There are two confirmations of this theory, both written in the nineteenth century in books on the history of English costume.

Mr A. Strutt writes in *English Dress*, vol: 1 'From the short tunic of the Saxon originated I doubt not the garment so commonly known to be worn at this day by the rustics in all parts

of England with the name of the "round frock". The collars and the wrist bands of such frocks are curiously decorated with needlework and in the same manner as we see the Saxon tunica ornamented.'

Mrs Ashdown in her book *British Costume During Nineteen Centuries* suggests 'it is perfectly permissible to suppose that the smock frock and the carter's gown of the present day with its peculiar needlework may be a direct descent of the Saxon "tunica".'

In Classical times the same garment was worn by all classes of society, but differences in social class were reflected in the texture of the woven fabric; the smock of the peasant was of a coarser material than the fine linen used by the nobility, who even coated the fabric with oil to give it the appearance of silk. This gloss finish is referred to by Homer in the *Odyssey* (Book XIX) 'I noticed his tunic too, it gleamed on his body like the skin of a dried

1 and **2** *Nineteenth-century smocks*

3 *Peasants wearing the* tunica *from a Saxon manuscript,* C. AD *700.* (BY COURTESY OF THE TRUSTEES OF THE BRITISH MUSEUM)

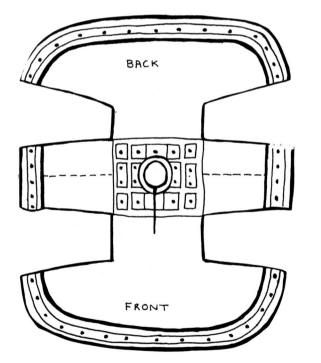

BACK

FRONT

4 *The* tunica, *originally of Roman origin, but still being worn in Saxon times*

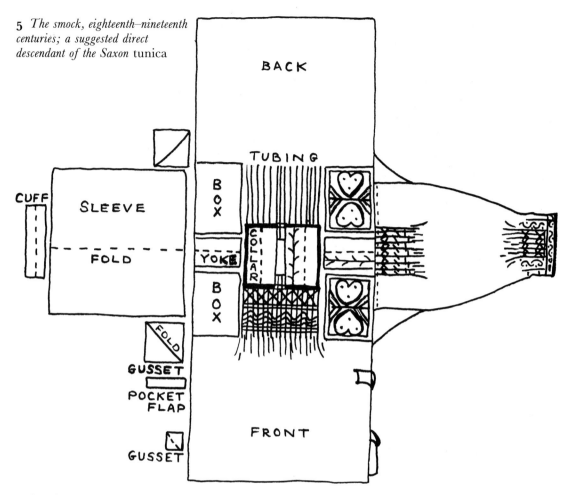

5 *The smock, eighteenth–nineteenth centuries; a suggested direct descendant of the Saxon* tunica

onion, it was smooth and it shone like the sun'. This oil treatment also enhanced the folds of the material as is seen to perfection in Greek sculpture.

As the Roman *tunica* developed into a more smock-like garment it is very interesting to note that the ornamentation in both colour and in design started to become an art form. Dyeing with natural dyes from lichens and other hedgerow plants produced cloth of many different hues to be made up into the *chiton* and the *kalobus* which were two styles of tunic worn by both sexes from 600 to 146 BC all over the Classical world and by all classes of society.

Under Imperial Rome the lavish ornamentation worked on the *toga* was in keeping with the extravagance of the life of the period. This over-elaboration had disappeared by the second century AD by which time the *tunica alba* had superseded the toga. The peasantry, meanwhile, continued to wear the short tunic. The *tunica alba* was still a simple long white robe but instead of being gathered in at the waist by a girdle, the fullness was fitted into a band round the neck, embroidered with a border design (7) which was repeated at the end of the sleeves. Additional embroidery in the form of discs was applied onto the shoulders and above the hem; these discs were known as *segmenta* (8).

The *clavus* (9) was a fashion of particular interest in its display of stripes of embroidery. At first the stripes were applied from the

9 *Tunic with* clavi *at shoulders, hem and cuffs*

6 *The short smock, from a cycle illustrating 'the tasks of the months' by Luca della Robbia, 1445.* (VICTORIA AND ALBERT MUSEUM)

7 *Border design, fifth century*

8 *The* tunica alba

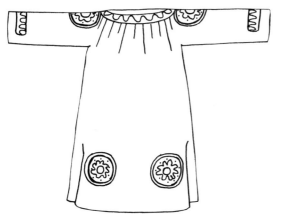

shoulder to the hem, but later they were shortened to extend only over the chest and were repeated as a border pattern along the hem and again at the cuff. Under Byzantine influence these shortened stripes became a form of decoration to denote distinction of office or status and in a similar manner to the heavy embroidery on the nineteenth-century smock they may have had a functional advantage in giving extra strength and protection where most needed.

Manuscripts of the Anglo-Saxon period, often illustrated with various types of illumination, depict figures drawn with vivid vitality. Some of the most charming of these illustrations represent pursuits such as ploughing and sowing in which the labourers can be seen wearing the Anglo-Saxon tunic.

Although the smock had its prototype far back in the history of costume, it has been seen to evolve in various ways over the centuries. It is recognized as a general trend in the history of costume that when the poorer classes of society start to adopt a fashion, the nobility change to something different and this seems to have happened in the development of the peasant smock. Late in the eighteenth century the highly ornamented chemise (*10*) vanished from the wealthy lady's wardrobe and at the same time the nobleman's shirt, which had been extravagantly decorated,

10 *Portrait of Dorothea Meyer Kamengeisser by Hans Holbein the Younger, 1676. She is wearing a chemise with an elaborately embroidered neckline.* (OEFFENTLICHE KUNSTSAMMLUNG, BASEL)

became a simple garment. It was at about this time that the peasants were starting to smock the fullness of what had been to date a drab shirt-like tunic.

Certainly the nineteenth-century smock served to satisfy for country folk the three main reasons which first induced man to create clothes: it gave the wearer a feeling of correctness in spite of his poverty, it encouraged a natural sense of art and it provided protection from the elements in the most practical manner.

Now, late in the twentieth century, the smock with its decorative embroidery technique – smocking – has again become of considerable interest and popularity. While the original practicality of the smocking technique, to control fullness of fabric, remains the prime reason for the stitchery, it is possible to use smocking as a decorative art in its own right, and the later chapters of this book interpret smocking in a free, experimental style. This new and modern approach will offer the student of embroidery and the fashion-conscious young of today imaginative ideas still reminiscent of our rich inheritance of traditional design. With a good understanding of the basic principles of smocking, progress into the free and experimental field is the best way to keep its tradition fresh and alive.

Two

The Traditional Smock as a Folk Costume

In many countries a folk costume is a treasured family heirloom to be worn mainly on festive occasions and passed down from one generation to the next. England has no national dress, but the simple yet artistically attractive peasant smock which was created and worn by the English peasantry over a long period of time and is steeped in folklore and ornamented with motif designs of folk art, could well be regarded as an English folk costume.

Unfortunately, as with all aspects of folk life, very few details have been recorded; the historian has only comparatively recently realized that future generations might be interested in their peasant heritage. We are left to guess or to try to piece together the information given by the surviving samples of smocks which are now mostly housed in museums. These relate to a later period in the history of smocking, so one can only theorize as to why the sudden change from simplicity to elaboration was made by the peasant after years of disinterest in fashion. One possibility, however, is that the embroidered motifs may once have had a symbolic meaning.

If there is any foundation to the theory that the embroidered motifs found on the smocks once denoted the trade of the wearer, it would seem that this was only the case in the eighteenth century. This is confirmed by Ann Buck's detailed survey in her interesting article 'The Countryman's Smock' printed in *Folk Life* vol: I, 1963. Of 54 smocks examined for the survey, only nine were associated with a particular occupation – six shepherd's, one cowman's, one carter's and one gardener's. Miss Buck finds little support for the theory that different motifs and designs were used for the different trades, and it would seem much more likely that by the nineteenth century the

11 *James Stevens, a centenarian living in Tring in 1890. His smock is typical of those worn by country folk in the nineteenth century.*

12 *Detail from a Wiltshire shepherd's smock, 1840*
13 *The shoulder cape of a coat smock, with a star and spiral motif.* (FOLK MUSEUM, GLOUCESTER)

14 *Detail from a nineteenth-century festival smock. The V.R. and crown on the embroidered panel suggest a date of 1837, when smocks were worn for The Great Exhibition. An elaborately decorated smock of this type would only be worn on special occasions.* (FROM THE COLLECTION OF THE LATE MRS PARKER)

embroidery was merely an exercise in fanciful yet attractive decoration (12, 13, 14). The smocking shown in early prints and pictures is very indistinct but it is obvious that the smock as a highly functional garment was ornamented with loving care by hands more accustomed to heavy work.

Mop fairs (15) followed an ancient custom, the history of which dates back to Roman times; they encouraged a lively exchange of merchandise from abroad as well as throughout Britain. William Howitt records in *The*

16 *Sheep shearing.* (LUTON MUSEUM)

15 *A mop fair, with a shepherd dressed in a typical smock.* (LUTON MUSEUM)

Hall and the Hamlet, 1845, that the first things he saw at the fairs were the smocks 'hanging on a crossed pole at the end of a vendor's stall waving aloft like scarecrows in the wind'. Other country gatherings such as sheep-shearing (*16*) and the status meetings were held during the autumn for the purpose of hiring farm hands. William Howitt again writes, in his book *Rural England*, 'in many parts of the country they offer themselves standing shoulder to shoulder with the next,

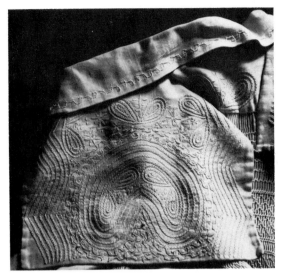

17 *The cape of a wedding smock, with intricate decorative stitchery.* (FROM THE COLLECTION OF THE LATE MRS PARKER. BY COURTESY OF WARWICKSHIRE MUSEUM)

18 *A Sunday smock. Traditionally there was little additional embroidery on these smocks, although this one has some decoration on the shoulders and collar.* (DORCHESTER MUSEUM)

the shepherd with his crook, the cowman with a twist of straw, and the carter a whip as his stock in trade held in his hand'.

There are several references to the smocks worn on particular occasions such as Plough Sunday, merry-making with Morris dancers, or at a wedding when the smock displayed a wealth of stitchery (*17*). Another old-time custom was for bearers at a funeral to be attired in long white smock frocks. A gift of eight such smocks was made to St Peter's Church at Hascombe near Godalming, Surrey, in 1898; each of these smocks has an inscription, a different phrase suitable for a funeral, embroidered on the collar. The Sunday smock has a character of its own; it was usually made up of a bleached linen with the ornamentation confined by tradition to the smocking or with the addition of very little embroidery; the lavishly smocked panels across the front and back of these smocks gave the attire the dignity called for as 'Sunday best' (*18*).

The various styles of smocks in England were possibly dictated by the part of the country in which they were worn; the fashion

19 *A cow gown or Sussex-style smock.* (GUILDFORD MUSEUM)

20 *A coat smock* (FOLK MUSEUM, GLOUCESTER)

appears never to have been adopted in Ireland or Scotland. It is interesting to try to trace the development of the shirt-like smock to the heavier coat-style, seemingly of a later date. The cow-gown or Sussex-style smocks (*19*) are almost primitive in their simplicity, and seem to be linked with the early history of the smock as a peasant's costume. There are several references to these simple smocks being worn in the south-east of England from 1797 to 1920.

The reversible frocks (*21*) so aptly described by Thomas Hardy as of 'pillow-case cut' were made up from several rectangular shapes as shown on the basic layout plan on page 41. The important part of the frocks was the ornamental and at the same time functional stitchery, the smocking, worked across the two panels of tubes gathered and smocked on the front and the back in identical manner. The fullness of the smocking was set into the shoulder straps and the collars from a slit opening at the centre front of the neck to a similar slit at the back so that the frock could be pulled over the head and worn either way round. Each side of the two smocked panels, surface embroidery was designed to fit into the 'boxes' which fill the area between the smocking and the underarm seams. The smocking and the embroidery together made these otherwise drab frocks into an artistic enterprise.

The coat style of smock, a much heavier type of garment, was more often found in the rural districts, being very suitable for labour in the fields and toil along the dirt roads (20). William Cobbett, the great benefactor of the peasant class, himself portrays farmhands on a visit he made to a Berkshire farm in 1821 as 'leather-legged chaps' for they were 'leather from sole to knee, then a pair of leather breeches, then a stout doublet, over this a smocked-frock so that the wearer sets bush and thorns and more at defiance'. The distinctive characteristic of the coat smock was the variation in the size of the collar, usually made up of several layers of material about 10 cm (4 in.) in width giving the effect of a cape over the shoulder. Alternatively, embroidered epaulettes extended into a series of tucks overlapping each other to give weight to the outer edge of this form of shoulder cape. So much thickness of thread and fabric must

21 *A reversible smock, with identical stitchery front and back.* (VICTORIA AND ALBERT MUSEUM)

22 *Epaulette of a smock worn by Squire Vaughan of Llanfilo, Breconshire, in the early nineteenth century.* (WELSH FOLK MUSEUM, ST FAGAN'S)

have added great strength and durability to the smock where it was most needed and given considerable protection to the wearer against wind and rain (*22*).

The pockets of all the styles of smocks were a significant feature; they varied in both shape and style as well as in size and in the way they were set into or onto the smock. They might be attached as patch pockets on the outside of the smock as shown in figure 21 or let into the inside of the coat horizontally across the side seams with a flap. On the reversible smock frocks the pockets were a simple slit left open in the side seams. The size of the pockets attached inside the smock was often considerable and they were known as 'poacher's pockets'.

The material used for the nineteenth-century smocks varied from the finer weight of shirt-like quality for smocks for leisure or for more festive occasions, to the heavy cotton twill, or duck, used on hard-wearing garments for work. Thomas Hardy refers to the fabrics of the smocks in *Far from the Madding*

Crowd, 1874, 'some were as usual in snow-white smocks and some in whitey brown ones of drabbet'. In the county of Radnorshire many of the farms grew flax, which was spun and woven by the family as a country craft into smocks either for their own use or to be sold to a trader who would pass them on to a customer, often some distance away, at the price of a labourer's full week's wage.

Coloured smocks were seldom seen. William Cobbett in *Rural Rides* declares 'such is the farm servant whether you see him in his white, his tawny, or his olive green smocked coat, in his straw hat or his wide-awake, all according to the prevailing fashion of the part of the country.' In *The Hall and the Hamlet* William Howitt refers to the colours worn in various counties of England and when he mentions the Midlands recalls the blue 'slop' style he had worn as a child. Even after comprehensive research and a study of the smocks which have survived to be housed in folk museums or private collections it is unfortunate to find that we still know more about the disappearance of the traditional smock than about its introduction.

Three

Folk Art and its Adaptation

Art has been an integral part of man's culture for many thousands of years; its original expression took the form of symbolic and naturalistic paintings, engravings and reliefs on the walls of caves. It is impossible to do more than surmise the purpose which these art forms served, but primitive art usually appears to fulful some practical role in the culture.

Figure 23 shows a spiral design on stone at Newgrange, Eire, possibly 4000 years old. Centuries later an Aylesbury smock (24) was decorated with a similar pattern. The recurrence of these primitive designs in later folk art must surely be an entirely accidental phenomenon resulting from the limited number of motifs that exist to be employed in pure design. However, many interesting comparisons can be made between the art forms and symbols found in modern folk art and those of pre-Christian times.

Aloris Riegl has written a thesis on the characteristics of folk art in which he suggests that it was 'primarily created by the humblest form of production to satisfy the needs of the home, independent of commercial gain'. When making these simple objects either for the home or for personal use, perfection was the peasant's aim because he knew that the more skill he put into the work, the better it

23 *A decorated stone from Newgrange, Eire, possibly 4000 years old.* (IRISH TOURIST BOARD)

24 *An Aylesbury smock with a spiral design*

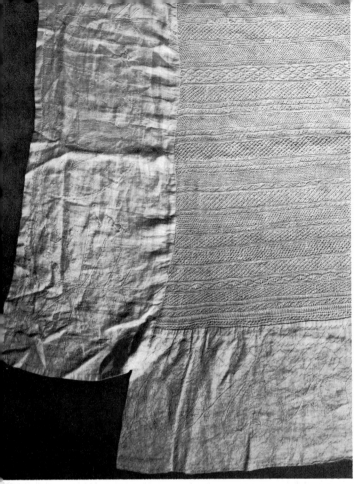

25 *An unusual smocked bed cover with embroidered side flaps.* (PHOTO: HALLAM ASHLEY)

26 *A Welsh round frock with a large shoulder cape* (ST FAGAN'S FOLK MUSEUM)

would serve its purpose. At the same time, the ornamentation of these day-to-day necessities gave the peasant an opportunity to exercise his natural creative instincts, with the result that his costume, his home and all it contained make an extensive and interesting study. There are several examples in the history of the smock that illustrate this point, such as an unusual type of bed cover, heavily smocked, with the side flaps embroidered with similar designs to those found on the traditional smocks (*25*) and a Welsh round frock with the large shoulder cape, a feature of the coat smock, instead of the small collar (*26*).

These objects produced by the country folk show the highest quality of craftmanship. Changes at this level of society take place very slowly, for the peasant was a natural conserver and styles of art were handed from one generation to the next. However, after a considerable length of time variations will occur and even the traditional patterns will be represented in a diversity of forms.

The designs on the English smocks all differ from one another, their variations being centred on a few basic stitches and shapes. With the use of only a coarse thread and fabric, the smock-makers showed real ingenuity and a keen attention to detail in creating such perfection in both the smocking and the embroidery. In this way the ornamentation on these purely functional garments was an expression of a living art and yet inextricably connected with past tradition.

Without colour, which always adds so

27 Embroidered epaulettes (SHREWSBURY MUSEUM)

28 The shoulder cape of a Shropshire smock, embroidered with heart motifs. (GALLERY OF ENGLISH COSTUME, PLATT HALL)

much gaiety and richness to folk costumes in many countries, the main interest in the English smock is the stitchery. Details of the basic smocking stitches, outline and cable stitch, are given in Chapter 4. The few stitches worked on the surface embroidery – chain stitch, feather stitch and French knots (*32*) – were used with amazing versatility on the motifs that made up the designs in the 'boxes', the shoulder capes and in less profusion on the collars, cuffs and shoulder straps.

As illustrated in Figure 27, there was a wide choice of shapes, which included circles, triangles, squares, ovals and cones. Other motifs represented flowers and leaves and

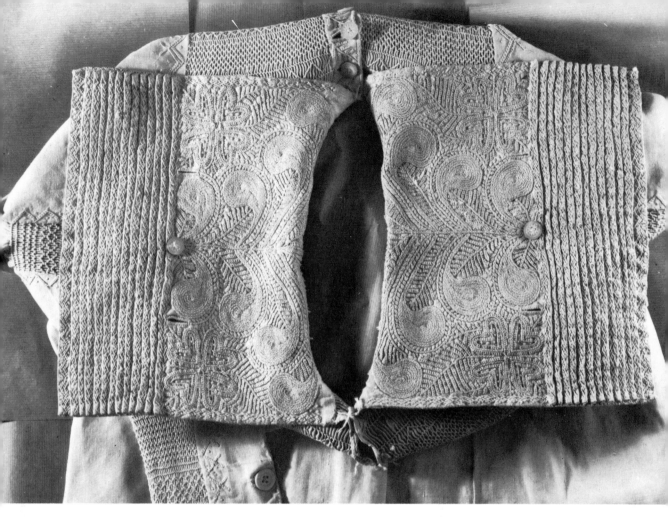

29 *A densely embroidered design; the extra thickness of the stitchery helped to strengthen the smock and protect it from wear.* (SHREWSBURY MUSEUM)

some had a symbolic suggestion such as the wealth of hearts (*28*). On some smocks a single shape predominates; in others several different motifs are combined and joined by interlacing or set in a framework of linear patterns.

Like the smocking, the surface embroidery had its practical use as well as its decorative charm. At times the stitchery was so dense that the background material completely disappeared (*29*). So much additional stitchery must have helped to strengthen the parts of the smock destined to receive punishing wear. The cotton or linen working threads may have been extracted from the material itself or hand-spun and dyed to shades of natural tone to match or contrast with the background.

The first mention of a family smocking business comes in 1826 in the Nottinghamshire town of Newark. The original patterns used by the firm were imprinted on metal blocks (*30*) from which subsequent prints could easily be transferred onto the fabric of what came to be known as the Newark Smocks (*31*). In every way the history of the traditional smock has been a lesson in adaptation as well as a source of folk art.

In the twentieth century, with the use of colour and many stitch variations, there is plenty of opportunity to enlarge on the past basic stitches and designs of traditional smocks. A combination of smocking and surface embroidery can be used to ornament many personal and household articles (*33 and*

30 *Blocks used in the Newark smock-making industry.* (GILSTRAP LIBRARY AND MUSEUM, NEWARK)

31 *Detail from a Newark smock embroidered with standard Newark patterns.* (WOODSPRING MUSEUM, WESTON SUPER MARE)

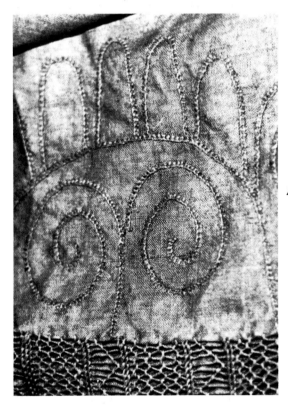

32 *Basic embroidery stitches used on nineteenth-century traditional smocks*

1 *Chain stitch*

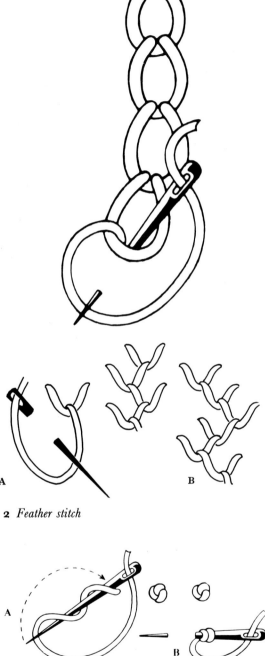

A   B

2 *Feather stitch*

A   B

3 *French knots*

33, 34 *The traditional designs and motifs used on smocks can be adapted for use on modern clothes and household articles*

embroidered with new, original designs worked in surface embroidery with a variety of stitches and colours to depict traditional motifs.

Simplicity was one of the most pleasing features in the basic folk designs used on the traditional smocks; their adaptation into the modern idiom offers a challenge to the inventive mind to achieve a pleasing effect, especially when one motif only is repeated several times (*colour plate 1*). On this apron the same colour scheme was carried out in the smocked panels worked to gather in the fullness at the waist. All the elements need to balance so that the surface is not too overcrowded; on the place mats (*34, 35*) the stitchery and the design are held together with interlacing and scrolling. These linear patterns give ideal scope for up-to-date stitch variation from the traditional theme of a few basic stitches.

colour plates 1 and 4). Basically the requirements are the same as when smocking and embroidery were worked together to ornament the peasant smocks in the eighteenth and nineteenth centuries, but the fundamental change today is rather in the way in which these objects have been influenced by superior materials. The free use of stitch and design with colour recreates the traditional ideas into a more modern approach as shown in the gay blouse and skirt designed for folk dancing (*colour plate 3*). The skirt is smocked into a waistband with an attachable embroidered belt; the yoke of the blouse and the wide border above the hem edge of the skirt are

35 *A set of four place mats. The linear designs can be worked in up-to-date stitch variations of the few basic stitches used on the traditional smocks.* (ŒNONE CAVE)

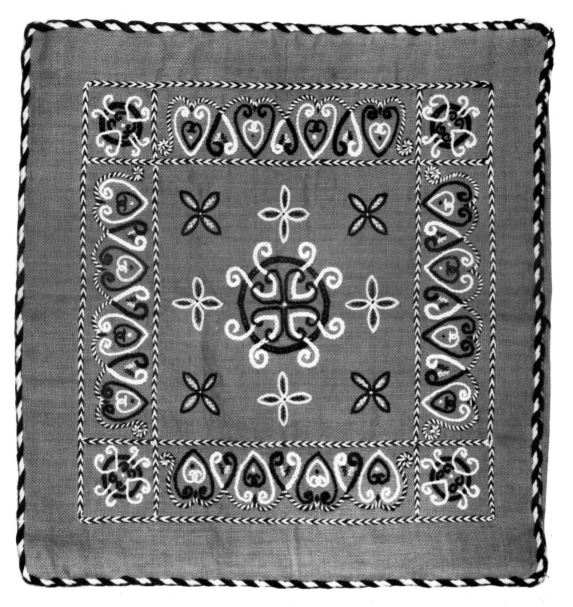

36 *A cushion cover embroidered in black and white in a mixture of cotton, silk and wool threads. The motifs are all derived from nineteenth-century smocks.* (ŒNONE CAVE)

The choice of material must depend largely on the purpose for which the object is to be used: a cushion cover needs to be of a heavier fabric than table linen, and the liveliness of colour looks attractive on a cushion so long as the correct proportion of light and dark tones are planned throughout the design. A full range of colours was selected to embroider the cushion cover (*colour plate 4*) designed to incorporate all the 'motifs' found during an extensive research of the nineteenth-century smocks. Textured threads and fabric can be used to great advantage; for the cushion cover in figure 36, only black and white silk, wool and cotton threads were used.

27

Four

Basic Smocking Techniques

Smocking is both a decorative and a practical technique which has been applied, in many ways, to fashion throughout the years of its popularity. Unfortunately it is not possible to trace exactly when smocking was first employed, although it is most likely to have been when the fashion for draped and tightly swathed garments changed to one of fullness. As with other traditional types of embroidery such as quilting and patchwork, smocking originated as a purely functional technique, in this case as a means of controlling fullness of material. Of all the ways of gathering material the method of smocked 'tubes' is undoubtedly the most practical, because while the material is held in place a certain amount of elasticity is retained.

There are many historical manuscripts, paintings and portraits which show garments gathered into bands, belts and yokes, but the actual stitchery is obscure. This omission on the part of the artist is understandable because the stitch which controlled the gathers was worked for its practical purpose only. The smocking stitch was inside the garment instead of ornamenting the outer surface and no doubt the brocade, a fabric worn at that time, needed no further embellishment. This method of smocking on the underside was used in controlling the gathers over the hips of the eighteenth-century robe to give the pannier effect.

The long skirt of the 1870s was smocked inside; the stitchery extended from the waistband nearly to the knee and the fullness then fell to the ankle in voluminous folds. This early method of controlling fullness from the inside may have been the basis for the modern approach of 'reverse' smocking as described on pages 86 and 87.

Babies' bonnets of an early period dis-played a great fineness of smocking and children's clothes in particular have for centuries been the subject of smocking reminiscent of Kate Greenaway's delightful illustrations. Even today a children's party is not complete without the added charm of at least one sample of this most attractive form of ornamentation for a child's party frock.

Smocking as a method of ornamentation worked over gathered tubes is a legacy from nineteenth-century traditional smocks (37). From one basic form of stitchery originally

37 *A panel of smocking on the back of a nineteenth-century coat smock.* (HEREFORD MUSEUM)

called rope stitch and now known as outline stitch, many interesting variations have been developed to give an additional attractive effect to the smocked designs. Outline, cable and wave stitch (*49: A,B,C*) are firmer in their hold of the tubes while diamond, honeycomb and vandyke stitch (*49: D,F,H*) tend to spread the fullness of the gathers. A carefully planned blending of the two groups of stitches with good spaces of plain tubing between the rows makes this basic functional stitchery beautiful in its adaptation.

MATERIALS

There is a wide range of materials which are suitable for traditional smocking and the choice depends on the type of article to be smocked. For children's clothes there is noth-

38 *A panel of smocking for the child's dress shown in colour plate 2.* (ŒNONE CAVE)

ing better than a lightweight wool, cotton or lawn; voile is attractive for infants. These fabrics are all soft, they hold the gathers well and splay nicely in the fullness below the panel of smocking (*38*). If a heavier background is required for a smock suitable for more casual wear, then the choice must depend on the price. Linen is ideal but it is expensive, and unbleached calico is a good alternative as it is hard-wearing and easy to launder. Calico needs to be of a good weight so that it will retain its crispness after it has been made up. When buying calico it is most important to include extra length to allow for shrinkage.

Colour is largely a matter of personal choice and as it plays an important part in the finished result, careful thought needs to be given to the type of article to be smocked, the working threads to be used and the background fabric. On a plain material the choice

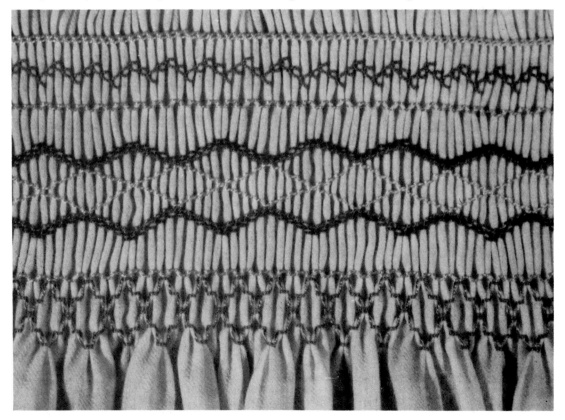

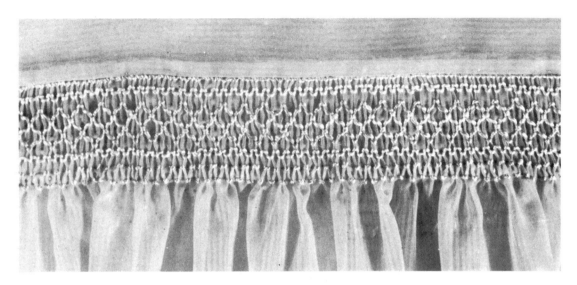

39 *Detail from an infant's dress smocked with silk thread on voile.* (ŒNONE CAVE)

and variation of the stitch is as important as the colour of the working threads. A pure white fabric smocked with threads in pastel shades gives a delicate effect for a young child's dress, and a plain background smocked with threads in tones of one colour only is a suggestion for a pair of rompers. A more lively look is achieved by using vivid colours on a contrasting background which creates an interesting effect for an older child's playsuit. Unless the pattern on the material is to be incorporated in the smocking plan (*48*) it is better to use a plain colour because it will show off the smocking to advantage. It is wise to avoid an all-over pattern in the background, however small, because the result becomes too fussy and spoils the identity of the smocking. Too many colours tend to interrupt the flow of the design; a good balance of light and dark throughout should be achieved.

The working thread used for the smocking needs to be in keeping with the background material. Silk ought to be used when smocking on silk and cotton on cotton. Select a fine thread for a delicate fabric and a heavy thread for a bold effect on a thick texture such as velvet. It is essential that the working thread has a good twist: coton à broder, cotton perlé no. 5 or no. 8, buttonhole twist or crochet cotton all retain the clarity of stitch when smocking. As well as the smocking thread it is important to use a good strong thread for picking up the dots (*42*). Synthetic polyester is to be recommended. It is also a help to pull the gathering thread through a piece of beeswax to give it additional strength and so avoid breakage.

FABRIC PREPARATION

Before commencing work it is necessary to prepare all fabric by pre-shrinking if it is not guaranteed pre-shrunk, straightening the grain so that the ends are at right angles to the selvedges and pressing to remove any wrinkles. To pre-shrink cotton or other washable fabric immerse it in hot water for about half an hour, drip dry and press. For wool, wet a sheet and place on a flat surface, lay the fabric on the sheet, roll them together and leave overnight. Unroll the fabric, leave it to dry and press if necessary using a steam iron or damp pressing cloth.

SPACING DOTS

Calculating the correct amount of material for a specified width of smocking is not easy, three times the width being only a general guide. The gathers on homespun linen used for peasant smocks could be picked up by the thread, but when the threads are too close to count, dots need to be used. An accurate way to be sure of good results is to work a sample using the same fabric, thread, and same spacing of dots as those chosen for the finished article. Measure across the panel of smocking dots with the material stretched out flat, then check the measurement after the sample has been completed; the number of dots used for the sample can be multiplied to fit the width and the depth of the final piece of smocking. The spacing of the dots both in width and in depth depends primarily on the weight of the fabric. The finer the fabric, the closer the dots need to be; dots spaced further apart will use more fabric, and the tubes will be deeper.

There are several ways to transfer the dots onto the material. Perhaps the best method is to mark the required width and depth of the dots onto a sheet of greaseproof paper. Pin the paper onto the wrong side of the material, making sure that the dots run on the straight grain of the fabric. Gather the dots up with a contrasting colour of thread directly through the paper; tissue paper is used when picking up the dots through a very fine or transparent fabric such as voile. After all the rows of dots have been gathered up, score along the lines of stitches with the point of the needle and tear away the paper. The alternative method of transferring the dots onto the material is to use the commercial sheets of dots that are ironed off onto the wrong side of the fabric. These sheets are obtainable with various spacing of the dots in both the width between each dot and the depth between each row; these ironed-off dots in blue, yellow or silver are sometimes not easy to wash out after the smocking has been completed, so when this method is used it is wise to pick up the last row of dots by eye.

Shaped yokes and curved lines may be required, in which case the pattern piece of dots needs to be slashed and spread to fit the shape (*40*). Points look attractive smocked in

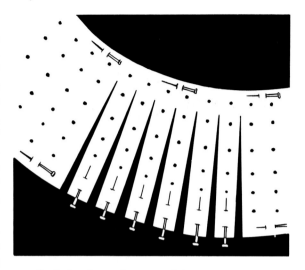

40 *Slashed and spread pattern of dots*

cable or honeycomb stitch (*49: B,F*) either as a filling design or worked as a finish to a panel of smocking; they help to splay the fullness and give a light effect to the folds of the fabric. The number of dots for a point needs to be calculated so that each row has one dot subtracted at each end with the last row consisting of three dots to make two tubes (*41*).

41 *Spacing dots for a point*

PREPARING THE TUBES
Gathering up the dots into tubes is the key to successful smocking; so often the most laborious stage of a process is in its preparation, yet this may be the most important part to assure good results. This is certainly so with smocking, as no perfection later will correct an inadequately controlled panel of tubes. Each

row of dots must be picked up with a separate thread. Check to make sure each thread is long enough to measure across the row of dots plus an extra 15 cm (6 in.). Make a good knot at one end of the thread and starting with a small back stitch, pick up each dot as evenly as possible (*42*) so that the depth of the tubes is equal.

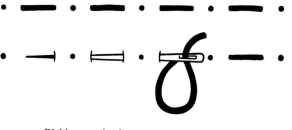

42 *Picking up the dots*

After all the rows of dots have been picked up, pull up the gathering threads in pairs and secure each thread round a pin in a figure-of-eight (*43*). It helps to push the fabric up the threads rather than pulling on the individual threads themselves, which are liable to break. The tubes need to be slightly more compact

43 *Gathering the tubes*

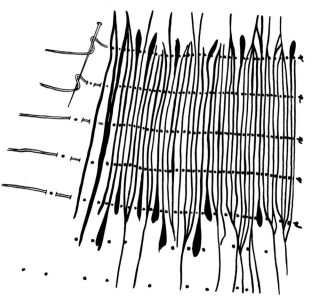

than the required width of smocking, as there is always a certain slackening of tension on the control of the gathers during the smocking. Stroke down the tubes with the eye of a needle as you progress to help set the tubes into a straight line.

If some of the threads seem to remain slack, reposition them before the smocking is started; if pins are used this is quite easy. If a large area of smocking is to be worked it is as well to secure the right-hand knotted side down with the pins onto an ironing board or a similar surface so as to provide a straight firm line when pulling up the tubes; this enables them to be set at an equal length. Check to compare the tension and measurement with the sample of smocking already worked.

THE SMOCKING DESIGN

Considerable thought needs to be given when planning the design of stitches to be smocked over a panel of tubing. It is often an advantage to chart the design onto a piece of squared paper before starting to smock the stitches onto the material (*44*). Work the plan from the centre outwards so as to create a good balance of stitch and spacing between the rows of smocking.

When smocking plain checks no dots are necessary; a beginner will find a straightforward checked fabric of two contrasting shades or colours an ideal way to learn and experiment with a variety of smocking stitches worked in a colour of thread contrasting to the colour of fabric, which is emphasized by gathering up the alternative checks (*45*). A checked material such as gingham is so colourful in itself that it is the stitch rather than the colour of the working thread that is important; the light and dark tones of the colours depend on the way the checks are gathered.

Squares, dots and stripes (*46*) on a fabric are a decoration in themselves. They are best used as the basis of the smocking design, and

44 *A design charted before working*

REPEAT

REPEAT

REPEAT

33

45 *Detail from a checked sunsuit in red and white cotton. Dots are not necessary for smocking on checked fabric.* (ŒNONE CAVE)

47 *Stitch sequence for smocking without dots on striped fabric*

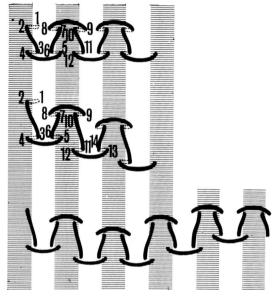

46 BELOW *Smocking over squares, stripes and spots*

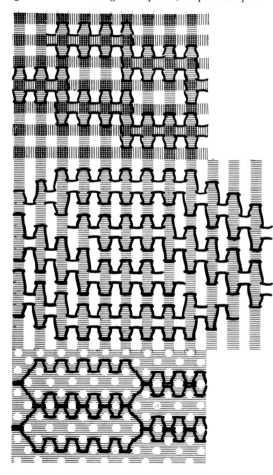

48 *Smocking on a patterned fabric, without working gathers first*

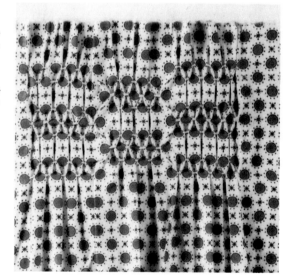

as for smocking checks, no dots are required. Instead of gathering the fabric into tubes, follow the stitch sequence shown in figure 47. Step the stitch across, up or down the dots, squares or stripes as freely as possible; after a little practice it is not difficult to judge an even stitch. This technique was used to gather up the fullness shown in figure 48; because so little smocking shows on the surface, honeycomb stitch was ideal as it did not detract from the background pattern which was incorporated in the freely smocked design.

STITCHES

As already mentioned, all the smocking stitches, with the exception of feather stitch, spring from the same basic source – outline stitch. Originally there were three main groups – rope, basket and chevron. Broadly speaking the variation of stitch is made by the thread being either above or below the needle. Figure 50 shows the formation and the names that the stitches have now acquired.

Always start smocking on the second row of gathers; the first row can be used in the making up of the garment. Outline or cable stitch are best to use at the heading of a panel of smocking because they add more rigidity to the gathers, whereas wave, diamond or vandyke stitches tend to spread the gathers and so are more suitably placed towards the lower part of the smocked panel. When all the smocking stitches have been completed do not remove the gathering threads until you have steamed the fabric. Use either a steam iron or a hot iron over a slightly damp cloth placed on top of the right side of the smocking; do not allow the iron to touch the gathers, as this may flatten the smocking.

Outline stitch (49A)

Alternate the thread below and above the needle while working each row of smocking. The spaces between the rows can be close together or evenly spaced apart.

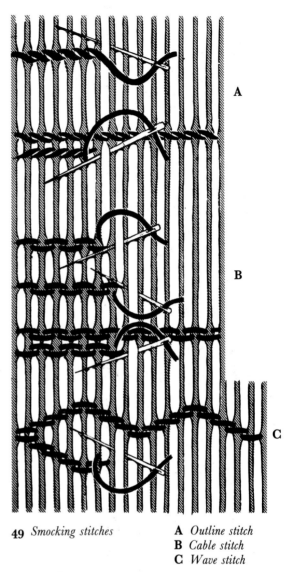

49 *Smocking stitches*
    A *Outline stitch*
    B *Cable stitch*
    C *Wave stitch*

Cable stitch (49B)

Bring the thread up to the left of the first tube. With the thread *above* the needle pick up the second tube from right to left; the third tube is picked up in the same way as the second but with the thread *below* the needle. Continue in this way, being sure to alternate the thread with each stitch until the row has been completed.

Wave stitch (49C)

This stitch is worked on the diagonal between

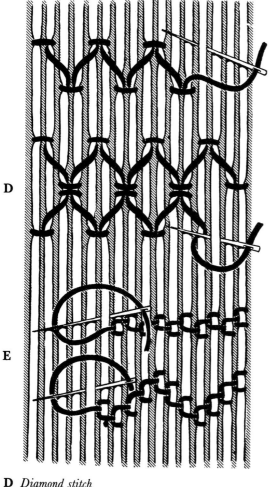

D *Diamond stitch*
E *Feather stitch*

Diamond stitch (*49D*)
Diamond stitch is worked between two gathering threads. Bring the needle out on the left of the first tube level with the top row of gathering threads; with the thread *above* the needle pick up the second tube; take the thread down to the next row of gathering threads to pick up the third tube; with the thread *below* the needle pick up the fourth tube and continue in this way to the end of the row.

Feather stitch (*49E*)
Work from right to left, picking up a tube with each stitch. Feather stitch is often introduced on the surface to neaten the sides of a panel of smocking or as a decorative stitch on the yoke, collars or cuffs of a smock.

Honeycomb stitch (*49F,G*)
This is effective when worked to considerable depth on a panel of smocking which does not require too much stitchery on the surface. Two rows are worked over at the same time; the thread is taken to the back of the tubes between the top and bottom stitch after the second insertion of the needle. Surface honeycomb is worked in the same way but the

two rows of gathering threads; it is worked on the same principle as cable stitch except that the thread is not alternated as often. Working down the gathers, bring the needle and thread up into the first gather, take in the second gather from right to left, take up the subsequent gathers, each a little below the line of the last stitch, keeping the thread above the needle, until the next line of gathering thread is reached; alternate the working thread from above to below the needle, and repeat the process of stepped stitches, this time going up the distance between the two gathering threads.

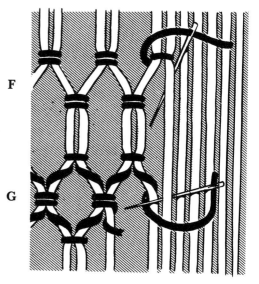

F *Honeycomb stitch*
G *Surface honeycomb*

thread carried between the rows of gathering threads appears on the surface instead of at the back of the tubes.

Vandyke stitch (49H)

Vandyke stitch is worked from right to left instead of from left to right. Two tubes are picked up with each stitch and are worked over twice. This is a strong stitch but it also has plenty of elasticity.

H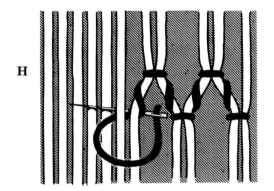

H *Vandyke stitch*

Five

Making Up a Traditional Smock

The return to fashion of the smock based on the nineteenth-century traditional style indicates that this historical garment still plays a part in modern life. Its practicality and the opportunity it offers for imaginative decoration make the smock and smocking as popular as ever, and they can be used in a diversity of ways. Figure 50 shows an excellent example of a traditional smock; the zigzag design is embroidered with feather stitch throughout (page 23); the smocking includes outline stitch, cable stitch and wave stitch (49); all four of these stitches are the original basic stitches worked on the majority of the nineteenth-century smocks.

50 *A traditional smock made in the nineteenth century*

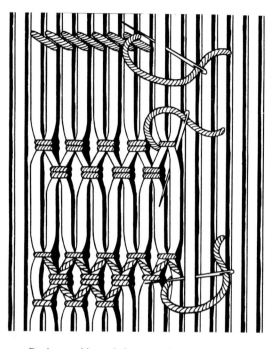

51 *Basic smocking stitches – outline, cable and surface honeycomb*

Today craft workers, artists and gardeners are happy to wear the smock frock in its original style (52) while the stylish young use it as a more personal expression. The wide choice of fabrics and experimental smocking techniques available make for variety and a new approach to a past tradition. In its basic form the smock is uncomplicated in its make up, economical in fabric and quick to assemble. The layout pattern (55) can be used for both the simple smock frock (52) or the more sophisticated coat style as worn in figure 53.

There are several details that have to be taken into consideration before the garment can be made up, and much depends on the intended use of the smock. Fabric is important: in spite of expense and the disadvantage

52 *Twentieth-century adaptation of the traditional smocked frock.* (ŒNONE CAVE)

53 *Twentieth-century adaptation of the traditional smocked coat.* (DAILY TELEGRAPH COLOUR LIBRARY)

of its creasing potential, linen is the ideal material for a smock as its weight encourages a good draping quality. Unbleached calico is an excellent hard-wearing fabric; however, its shrinkage when laundered is considerable and this has to be allowed for when assessing the amount of material required. The full

length of calico is best washed and ironed while still damp *before* the pattern is cut out so that it retains some of its crispness. Other alternatives are cotton drill or a light-weight denim; both are practical to wear and economical to buy. For a light-weight smock a good quality cotton polyester or tana lawn are suitable; for warmth viyella is recommended. For pure luxury a medium-weight silk noile can be used. Plain materials show off the smocking stitches to advantage, while the checks of gingham make interesting colour effects when gathered into tubes and smocked with an all-over stitch such as honeycomb. If colour is used, make sure that both the thread and fabric are fast-dyed because the smock is the type of garment which should be easy to launder either by machine or by hand.

When estimating the amount of material to buy, the length of the smock, the width of the fabric and the style should all be considered. Allow a total of 364 cm (144 in.) for an average-size smock cut from 90 cm (36 in.) fabric. If 115 cm (45 in.) wide fabric is used, the same quantity will be required, but for 150 cm (60 in.) fabric only 270 cm will be needed. The basic cutting plan (55) uses 306 cm (120 in.) by 90 cm (36 in.) plus an extra 60 cm (24 in.) to allow for working samples, normal shrinkage, bias bindings for the neck openings of the frock, front lacings and larger collars for the coat smock.

Trim off all selvedges and allow 1.5 cm ($\frac{5}{8}$ in.) for all run and fell seams and turnings. Use tailor tacks to mark top and bottom of folds and any other points which may be helpful when matching up the sections of the smock during the making up process. Following the cutting plan (54) fold together three sections of equal length 102 cm (40 in.) by 92 cm (36 in.) wide. Cut along the folds, having drawn a thread when possible, on the straight grain of the material. Put the remaining surplus 60 cm (24 in.) on one side for the extras.

CUTTING OUT

One of the three sections is for the front of the smock and one for the back; fold the third section in half lengthways and cut A and B. Fold section A into two halves for the sleeves; fold B into two halves and cut along the fold. From the double thickness of material cut out the following small sections: two collars 25.5 cm × 23 cm (10 in. × 9 in.); two underarm gussets 18 cm × 18 cm (7 in. × 7 in.); two side seam gussets 5 cm × 5 cm (2 in. × 2 in.); two cuffs 25.5 cm × 10 cm (10 in. × 4 in.); two shoulder straps 30 cm × 23 cm (12 in. × 9 in.). The two shoulder strap pieces have to be folded again to make four sections of 23 cm × 15 cm (9 in. × 6 in.). For the coat style, fold and cut the front body section lengthways into two halves for the front opening of the coat, in place of the 8 cm (3 in.) slit neck opening of the frock which is cut down during the making up process of the frock (step 3).

From the surplus length of material cut two narrow bias bindings for the neck opening of the frock style, one for the front and one for the back each 15 cm (6 in.) in length, or two front facings 5 cm × 92 cm (2 in. × 36 in.) for the coat style. Also cut out a slightly larger pair of collars for the coat style, 25.5 cm × 38 cm (10 in. × 15 in.), allowing 2 cm ($\frac{3}{4}$ in.) for each tuck.

WORKING THE SMOCKING

There will be ample material to cut out a good working sample to test the smocking techniques already given in Chapter 4. These can all vary according to the fabric, the thread and the style of smock to be made up. The most important point is to decide from working the sample on the dot spacing and the tension of the gathered tubes; the smocking stitches to be worked on the panels should also be tried out on the sample to see their effect and to check on their resilience. Dots spaced 1 cm ($\frac{3}{8}$ in.) apart along the rows and between the rows are an average gauge for a smock frock or coat-style smock. The smocking and the embroidery are worked *before* the sections of the smock are joined together.

Transfer the smocking dots onto the material by either of the two methods explained on page 31. The dots should be in panels 51 cm × 25.5 cm (20 in. × 10 in.) across the

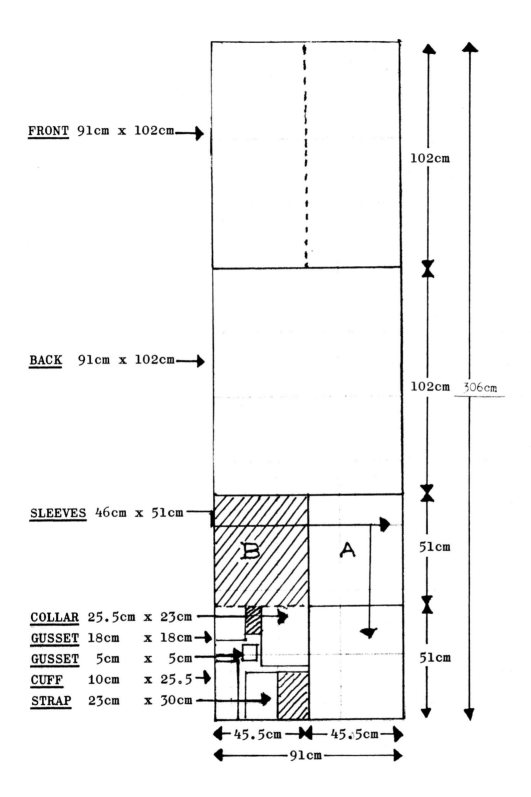

FRONT 91cm x 102cm ➝

BACK 91cm x 102cm ➝

SLEEVES 46cm x 51cm ➝

B

A

COLLAR 25.5cm x 23cm ┄
GUSSET 18cm x 18cm ➝
GUSSET 5cm x 5cm ➝
CUFF 10cm x 25.5 ➝
STRAP 23cm x 30cm ➝

102cm

102cm 306cm

51cm

51cm

◄─45.5cm─►◄─45.5cm─►
◄──────91cm──────►

centre of the front and back sections, starting the first row of dots 2 cm ($\frac{3}{4}$ in.) below the top raw edge, 13 cm × 10 cm (5 in. × 4 in.) at the top of the two sleeves and 36 cm × 9 cm (14 in. × $3\frac{1}{2}$ in.) above the cuff edge. Work the embroidery on the sections which are not going to be smocked before picking up the smocking dots. Draw the designs to be embroidered onto greaseproof paper and pin and tack each design into position – either side of the panels of dots on the front and back sections, on the shoulder straps, on the collars and the cuffs. With small running stitches taken through both the paper and the fabric, transfer the designs where they are required and then score along the lines of stitches and tear away the paper. Embroider the designs with feather stitch, chain stitch or one of the many variations of these two traditional stitches.

After the embroidery has been completed pick up the smocking dots with a strong,

bright-coloured contrasting thread; gather the threads into panels of tubes approximately 16 cm (6 in.) in width across the centre of the back and front, 4 cm ($1\frac{1}{2}$ in.) at the top of the sleeves and 10 cm (4 in.) at the cuff edge. So that the 8 cm (3 in.) slit opening at the centre front and back of the neck of the frock can be cut down *after* the gathering and smocking has been completed, the first few rows of dots are picked up in two halves to within 2 cm ($\frac{3}{4}$ in.) of the centre tack line. For the coat style the smocking is worked on both halves of the front to within 6 cm (2 in.) of the raw edges of the front opening. No opening is made at the back of the coat.

Before starting to make up the smock place all the sections into position ready to be joined together (55), so as to check that all 16

55 *The basic rectangular sections of the smock, cut out and placed in position. The smocking should be worked before the garment is assembled*

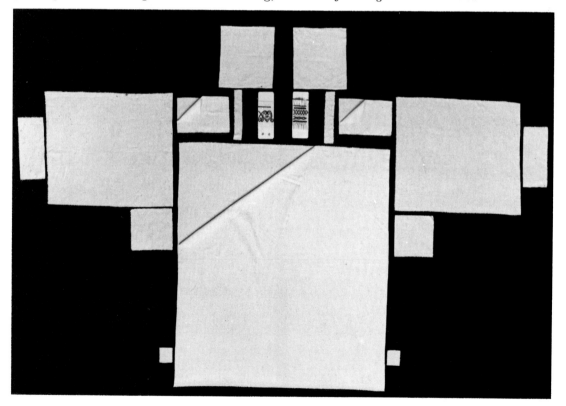

rectangles cut from the basic layout pattern (*54*) are correctly assembled. When the embroidered designs have been worked, the smocking on the panels of tubing has been carried out and the number of pattern sections have been checked, then you are ready to make up either the smock frock or the smock coat.

56 *Joining the shoulder strap to the front and back. The shaded areas represent the right side of the fabric*

MAKING UP

1 Fold the front and back sections in half lengthwise. Tack an 8 cm (3 in.) line down from the top of the folds to mark the front and back neck openings.

2 To join the shoulder straps to the front and back of the smock (*56*): pin, tack and stitch the right side of the strap to the right side of the front and the right side of the strap *facing* to the wrong side of the front (*A*). Turn to the inside of the smock (*B*). Turn the three

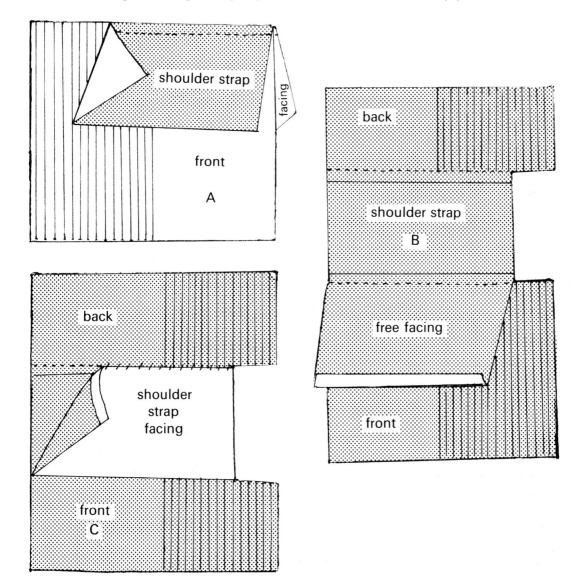

turnings joined together in figure 56A towards the strap and press. Pin, tack and stitch the right side of the strap to the right side of back; press the two turnings towards the strap and press. At this stage the strap facing is left free. Turn up the unattached edge of the facing, take the facing piece over the wrong side of the strap and slip stitch the fold of the turned-in edge to the line of stitches which attached the strap and back together (C).

3 For the smock frock cut the 8 cm (3 in.) centre front and back neck openings, marked with the tacking lines; neaten the raw edges of the openings with the 15 cm (6 in.) bias bindings. First join the right sides together, then turn the bias facing to the inside and slip stitch the turned-in edge to neaten. For the coat style attach the 5 cm (2 in.) front facings to the full length of the two front halves of the smock and stitch with right sides together. Turn the facings to the back and slip stitch the turned-in raw edges of the facings at the back.

4 Fold the 25.5 cm × 23 cm (10 in. × 9 in.) collar in half right sides together, join the short ends with a small turning, turn the collar to the right side and press. Pin the centre of the collar to the centre of the shoulder strap and the two ends to the neck bindings. Tack and stitch with right sides together the front, strap, back and collar to join. Repeat the same process with the second collar taking care not to flatten the panels of smocking at the front and the back of the smock. Turn the collars over to the wrong side and slip stitch the turned-under raw edge to the inside stitching line. For the coat smock join the larger collars in the same way as the small collars on the frock, *after* the two tucks have been stitched either side of the outer fold, on the right side; these tucks not only look attractive, they also add weight to the set of the larger collars over the shoulders.

5 Fold the two sleeves in half lengthways and mark the top and the bottom of folds, and the underarm raw edges with tailor tacks 15 cm (6 in.) down from the top and 8 cm (3 in.) up from the bottom. Open out the sleeves and

with the right sides of the front, strap, back and sleeve together, pin, tack and stitch together, matching the centre of the panel of smocking at the top of the sleeve to the centre of the shoulder strap. Join the other sleeve in the same manner, taking care not to flatten the smocking.

6 The sleeve and side, run and fell seams can be stitched by hand or by machine; the insertion of the underarm gusset is best carried out by hand. With the right sides of the sleeves together, tack and stitch the run and fell seam leaving the openings for the gusset and the wrist hem as marked by the tailor tacks. Join the front and back sections of the smock with run and fell seams leaving openings at the top for the underarm gussets and a 23 cm (9 in.) slit opening up from the hem edge, as marked by tailor tacks. Layer the seams to remove the bulk.

7 Insert the gusset into the underarm opening (57), 15 cm (6 in.) down the sleeve seam edges and 23 cm (9 in.) down the side seam edges, matching the tailor tacks. Pin the four corners of the gusset to the four seams; continue the run and fell seams stitched to join the sleeves and the sides together along the four sides of the gusset so as to join it in neatly at the underarm position.

8 Neaten the 8 cm (3 in.) wrist opening with a narrow hem. Fold the cuff in half with right sides together, join the short ends with a small turning, turn the cuff to the right side and press. With the right sides of the cuff and the sleeve together pin, tack and stitch together, taking care not to flatten the smocking. Turn the cuff to the inside of the sleeve and slip stitch the turned-back raw edge to the stitching line. Join the other cuff and sleeve in the same way. Work small buttonholes on the overlap edge of each cuff and attach the buttons at the other end to match.

9 Turn in a narrow hem to neaten the two slit openings at the bottom of the side seams. Turn in and tack the raw edges of the small gussets, place them over the side seams at the top of the slit openings and slip stitch the

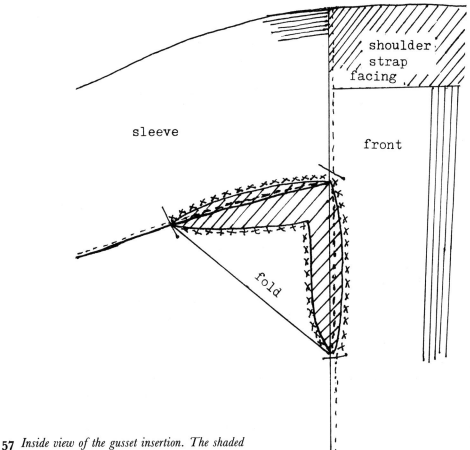

sleeve

shoulder
strap
facing

front

fold

57 *Inside view of the gusset insertion. The shaded areas represent the right side of the fabric*

gussets into position so as to strengthen the joins.

10 Turn up a hem and stitch it on the inside to make the smock the required length. Sew the buttons equally spaced down the double thickness of the under front facing of the coat smock; mark the exact position for the buttonholes with parallel lines of tacking very slightly wider than the diameter of the buttons at right-angles to the outside edge of the outside facing.

11 Remove all the tailor tacks and any tacking threads, and steam-treat the smocked panels before taking out the gathering threads. Press the whole smock with a hot iron to firm up the folds below the tubes and to show off its attractive appearance.

Six

The Modern Approach

Earlier chapters have traced the history and development of smocking in its traditional setting of peasant-style costume and children's clothes. The craftsmanship and intrinsic beauty of the garments made in the traditional manner will always be admired; and traditional smocking will always have a rightful place among the basic skills of the professional embroiderer. However, it is quite unnecessary to view the art of smocking as something which belongs only to the past. In the second part of this book we hope to show the reader that smocking is indeed alive and well and is as relevant and exciting today as it was in the past. This does not mean disregarding tradition and changing to new ideas at any cost; rather it is the skilful blending of the traditional with the new to achieve a total effect which will be admired by future generations as we admire the best work from the past.

So often one hears the comments 'My children are much too old to wear smocking now' or 'My figure is the wrong shape for smocking' or, perhaps worst of all, 'It is old-fashioned and so limited'. Old-fashioned and limited it most certainly is not and it is no longer necessary to think of smocking purely in terms of gathers on children's clothing or adults' smocks. The traditional smock can be a most versatile and beautiful addition to any fashionable wardrobe but, once the technique and a few basic stitches have been mastered, it is possible to find many other ways of including this exciting form of embroidery. The visual impact and decorative quality of smocking, which depends on lines and their distortion, can be used to advantage on a wide variety of garments for practical and decorative wear. This is reflected in the way in which many of the top fashion designers are using smocking to enhance dresses where fullness is an important part of the style. It could be used as a background for further embellishment with beads, semi-precious stones or surface embroidery on the bodice of a rich ball gown. A quilted jacket could have areas of smocking included to give textural contrast as well as added warmth and protection. Delicate stitchery can be introduced into lingerie. A filmy nightdress or negligée made from Swiss lawn, fine silk, satin or polyester could be made to look even more alluring by using the simplest of stitch designs. The addition of smocked panels, worked either in a matching thread or a range of colours, on the sleeve, cuff or skirt can transform the simplest dress or turn a christening robe into a family heirloom. It is even possible to give an air of romance to a plain ready-made blouse or dress by the addition of smocked bands or insertions as will be explained in a later chapter.

Fabrics, threads, colours and designs suitable for traditional smocking have already been described in Chapter 4. These are now repeated where necessary and extended to introduce a modern approach.

CHOICE OF FABRIC

A wide variety of fabrics such as silk, cotton, wool, fine jersey, satin, synthetics and fine leather can be used for modern smocking, as experimentation will show. If they are to be incorporated into fashion, fabrics need to be soft, pliable, to drape well and to be of a suitable weight and type for the style of garment to be made. If the style requires a lot of fullness, choose a lightweight fabric as it will drape and mould to the body. Sheer fabrics such as chiffon and organza will also smock beautifully but do require expert handling using very fine thread with the stitches accurately and neatly placed. To retain the delicate effect of the fine fabric the more open and lacy stitch combinations of smocking stitches are advisable. Heavier-weight fabrics such as needlecord, velvet and double jersey will also smock effectively but a deeper tube needs to be used.

Striped fabric

Stripes on a fabric to be smocked can display great versatility when used with imagination. Panels can be set in with the stripes running in different directions to bring out a special design feature. Honeycomb smocking worked over the lighter of the two stripes will give a strong three-dimensional look. When using the fabric in this manner, you may find it quicker and easier to bring the stripe forward if the gathering thread is stitched from stripe to stripe instead of picking up a small quantity at each dot; to do this, insert the needle into the edge of one stripe and bring it out at the next until the row is complete.

Patterned fabric

Patterned as well as plain fabric can be used in many different ways but remember that when an all-over patterned fabric is gathered, both the colour and the pattern will change. It is therefore advisable to work a sample first and to choose the colour of thread for smocking after the fabric has been gathered. Too many colours will cause confusion and loss of impact, so limit the choice to one or two. A simple stitch such as honeycomb or diamond may be more suitable than a complicated design.

THREADS

Twisted threads such as perlé no.5 or no. 8, coton à broder and silk or polyester buttonhole twist are recommended as they are strong and less likely to shred than the stranded variety. The stitches will stand out well with a crisp finish. Crochet cotton, lurex, knitting wools and random-dyed yarns can also be considered whilst experiments with more unusual threads and ribbons can produce exciting results. Several kinds of thread can be used in the same piece of work to give added interest.

GATHERING MACHINES

The accurate gathering and preparation of the fabric for smocking can be tedious but, as has been stated in earlier chapters, it is essential for a well finished result. To assist this preparation there are gathering machines on the market which may be worth considering if a great deal of fine smocking is to be undertaken. The machines do, however, have their limitations regarding the depth of tubes being gathered. One area where they can be an advantage is where gathering for a textural effect only is required. A crisp fabric such as cotton will hold the pleating well, whereas the springier polyesters can have a bubbly ruched appearance owing to the shallow tubing the machine gives. This bubbly effect could be exploited and is worth further development, especially for use in panels, hangings or for pure ornamentation.

STITCHES

The basic stitch techniques used in smocking have already been described in Chapter 4 but it is possible to extend these in a number of ways to give added variety and interest and to allow individual designs or motifs to be developed. The motifs thus created can be used in groups or isolated in 'spots' as an ideal way of introducing a small touch of contrasting colour to a scheme and adding punch to the overall effect.

Satin stitch (58)

This is a particularly useful stitch for adding an extra touch of colour or weight to a 'thin' design. Start by bringing the needle up at the left-hand side and, taking between two and four gathers together, make horizontal stitches one above the other until the desired space is filled.

Bullion stitch (59)

This stitch can be worked singly or in groups.

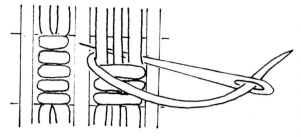

58 *Satin stitch*

Three stitches worked together will make attractive rosebuds with small detached chain stitches added as leaves. Practice and patience are needed to master this stitch but the result can be very worthwhile. Working over four gathers, bring the needle out on the left-hand side of the first left-hand tube. Then insert it horizontally four gathers to the right to form a back stitch, bringing the needle point out in the left-hand gather where it first emerged. Do not pull the needle right through the fabric. Twist the thread round the thick part of the needle close to where it emerges from the material. Seven or eight twists are about the number needed to equal the length of the back stitch but this should be varied according to the thickness of material and thread used. Hold the left thumb on the coiled thread and gently ease the needle and thread through. Still holding the coiled thread, turn the needle back to where it was inserted in the side of the right-hand tube and push it to the wrong side at the same place.

59 *Bullion stitch*

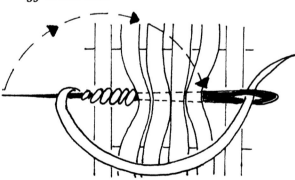

Pull the thread through until the bullion stitch lies flat.

If the coils should become loose or tangled whilst the thread is being pulled through, a few strokes with the needle between the twists and the thread will smooth them out.

Cable stitch
Small flowerettes (60)
Small detached groups of cable stitch are used to make up the flowerettes. They can be particularly effective when worked in the middle of trellises or used for adding small areas of extra colour to give impact to a design. Each flowerette is worked over four gathers. Work three cable stitches with the thread alternately below and above the needle, then from the end of the third stitch bring the needle back up to the right of the third tube and take a level stitch to the left of the second tube with the thread below the needle. Fasten off neatly at the back.

Threads can run up and down the tubes but should not run across the tubes at the

60 *Small flowerette*

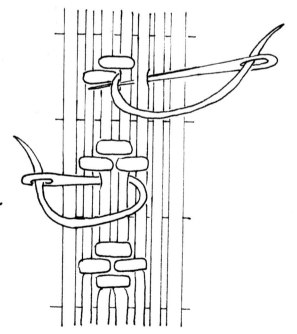

1 *A smocked apron with a matching border embroidered in traditional surface stitchery.*
Made by Œnone Cave.

2 *A child's viyella dress smocked in yellow and two shades of blue. The stitches used are outline, feather, cable, wave and surface honeycomb.*
Made by Œnone Cave.

3 Blouse and skirt designed to be used for folk dancing. The skirt is smocked into a waistband with an embroidered belt attached. The yoke of the blouse and wide border above the hem of the skirt are embroidered with original designs of surface stitchery to depict traditional motifs in a modern idiom. Made by Œnone Cave for Sheena Squibbs.

4 A cushion designed to incorporate all the motifs found during an extensive research of surviving nineteenth-century smocks.
Made by Œnone Cave.

5 *Spray painting over triple honeycomb-smocked*
   white satin on the cuffs, yoke insert and
   headdress adds a romantic touch to a simply
   styled wedding dress.
   Made by Jean Hodges for Caroline Dedman.
   (Photo: Mike Farmer)

6 *Detail of Waterfall panel showing surface smocking with the addition of hand and machine embroidery.*
Made by Ros Chilcot.

back. It is best to finish off the threads on each individual motif unless they are being worked close together. Threads running across the back can easily get caught up or, more important, alter the elasticity and shape of the work.

Baskets (61)

An attractive flower basket motif can be worked by using double cable stitch which, when worked in a block, resembles the weaving on a basket. The handle is depicted by satin and stem stitch. Flowers can be added with detached chain stitch or suitable surface stitchery in textured threads for extra interest. Baskets can be worked as single motifs or in a row.

The basket is worked over 18 tubes and five gathering threads although the actual number of gathering threads can vary depending on the depth of dot being used. Starting on the third gathering line work 17 cable stitches. Continue downwards using cable stitch and work one less stitch at the beginning and end of each successive row until there are seven stitches. The fabric is turned to enable the stitching to continue backwards and forwards across the rows. To make the base of the basket work another row of seven stitches and then a final row of nine. The handle is shaped by working satin and stem stitch as shown in figure 61.

Many pictorial designs and scenes such as

61 *Basket*

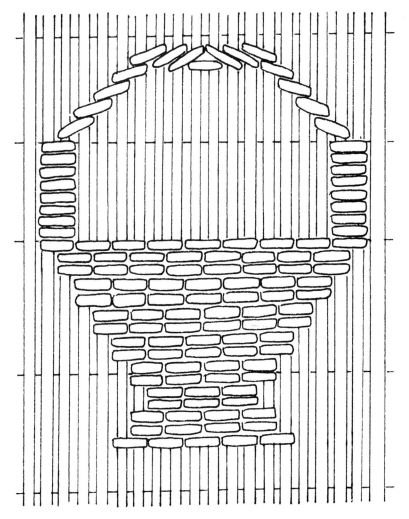

49

houses, trees, vehicles, people and animals can be devised by stacking stitches to make squares and pyramids to bring a new and exciting dimension to the work. Parallel rows of cable stitch will produce square shapes whilst opposite rows will produce pyramids. These free designs can be drawn on the fabric by pulling the gathering threads tight to close up the tubes and marking with tailor's chalk. Basic stitches are then used to work the design with added surface embroidery stitches if required. Blocks of colour can also be created in this manner.

When making pictorial scenes or designs, the areas where there will be no actual smocking to keep the tubes in place must be held by reverse smocking. This means working rows of cable or honeycomb stitch on the back of the fabric to prevent the tubes distorting and flattening (see page 87).

Stitch variations
An individual approach can be created by combining different stitches within a row

62 *Square and pyramid*

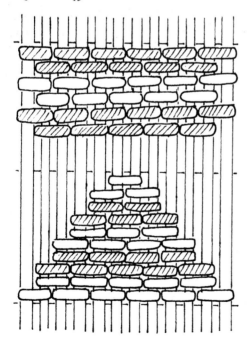

such as a group of about seven cable stitches followed by one or two diamond stitches. If this is repeated, interesting geometric patterns can be produced.

Trellis stitch variations can be devised by varying the number of tubes used on each or alternate trellises (*63*). A half-space wave followed by a full-space wave then a half-space again will form a diagonal pattern (*64*).

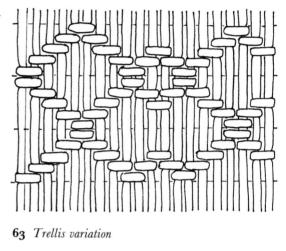

63 *Trellis variation*

64 *Diagonal wave*

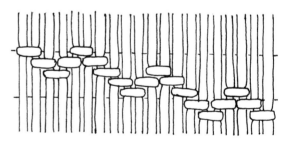

Vandyke stitch can be used in a similar way to give a more spiky appearance (*65*). Likewise, stem or wave stitch can be made to travel in different directions by turning the work upside down, thus creating a pattern build-up. Scrolls and swirls using chain or stem stitch can also be worked provided the tubes are held in place on the back.

Honeycomb stitch can make a perfect background for further development. A dress for a child or adult could be imaginatively

65 *Diagonal vandyke*

66 *Diagonally worked honeycomb stitch.* (MARGARET ROBERTSON)

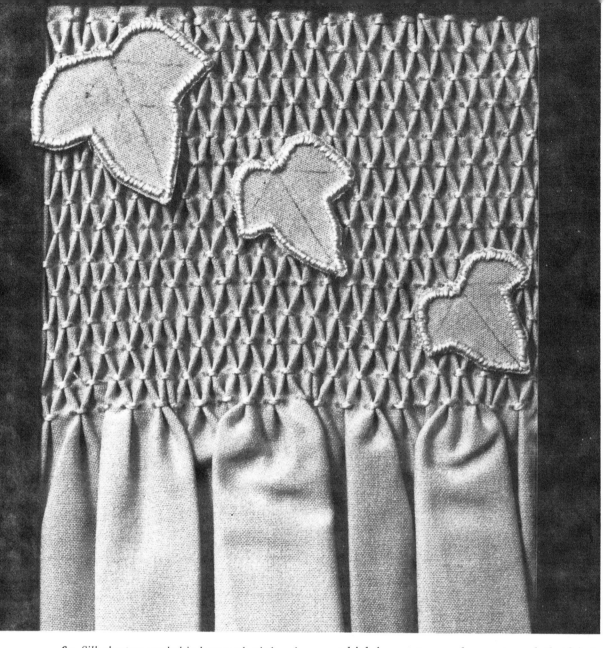

67 *Silk shantung worked in honeycomb stitch makes an ideal background for the applied leaves.* (EILEEN PLUMBRIDGE)

decorated by means of applied leaves, flowers or shapes. These can be formed by joining two fabrics together with Bondaweb, cutting to shape, stitching the edges by hand or machine and then applying the shape to the gathers. (Bondaweb is a soft, iron-on adhesive web which is easy to use, does not mark the fabric and is available, ready packed, in most haberdashery departments.) Many creative ideas can be produced by taking various numbers of folds together and working random honeycomb stitch. Triple honeycomb is yet another interesting variation with the free tubes giving a feeling of movement.

Pointed smocking can be used in many ways on a variety of garments and articles. Points of varying size could radiate down a skirt or dress to give an interesting hip line; they could extend from the cuff up the sleeve; from the neck line over the shoulder; in a panel down the front of the bodice reminiscent of a stomacher or, in fact, any suitable placing where the features will enhance the appearance. Points can also be used to give focal interest to the gathers around a bed valance or at the top of a decorative curtain.

Stitch designs

The combination of stitches used will hold the tubes open or closed to form varying patterns. These background patterns, as well as the actual stitches, should be observed and taken into account when building up a design. If all the stitch rows are crammed together the background pattern will be lost and with it the intrinsic beauty and elasticity of this embroidery technique. Likewise, too many different stitches can cause a fussy and restless effect, so avoid the enthusiastic inclusion of every known stitch in one piece. It is better to use three, or possibly four, basic stitches and rely on the way in which they are combined to achieve an interesting design.

COLOUR

Particular attention should be paid to the choice of colour scheme as it is a very important aspect of smocking. In view of the general linear effect of the stitches, colours cannot always be blended in quite the same way as in other forms of embroidery. This is one reason why the number of colours used within a piece of work should be carefully considered and chosen in advance. Too many colours can have a restless, jazzy appearance, thus ruining the main concept of the technique. It must also be remembered that the shapes made by the tubes in the background are important and should not be obscured by the overwhelming impact of colour.

A subtle textural effect can be obtained by using a self colour such as a green thread on a matching green fabric. A monochromatic scheme can be used with tints, tones and

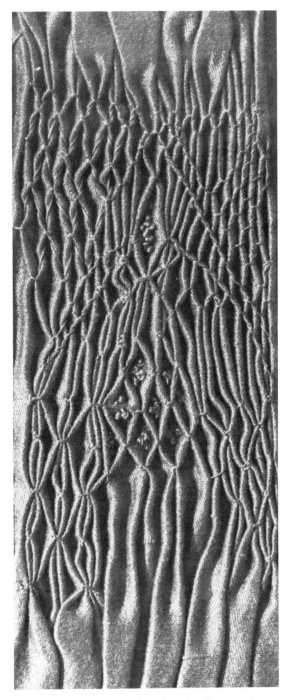

68 *A sample of honeycomb and surface honeycomb stitch worked at random to illustrate some of the variations these stitches can produce.* (SONJA HEAD. PHOTO: ANDREW HODGES)

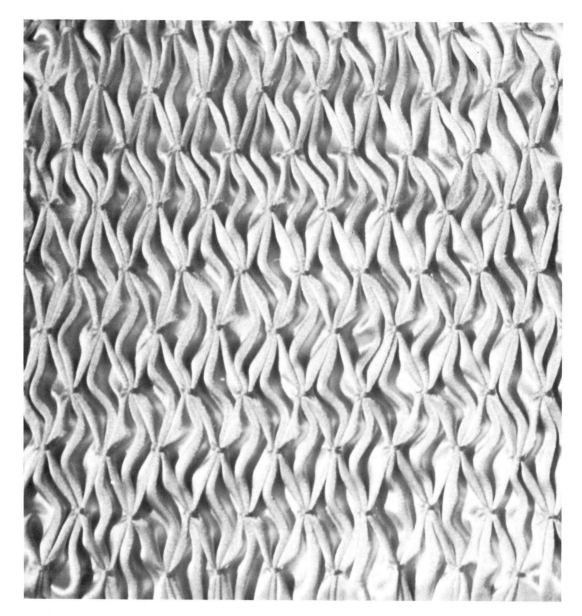

69 *The richness of triple honeycomb stitch worked on satin also gives a feeling of movement.* (JEAN HODGES)

70 *Surface honeycomb stitch worked over striped fabric creating a three-dimensional look. Pointed smocking can be used effectively on a variety of garments and articles.* (SUE LACKIE)

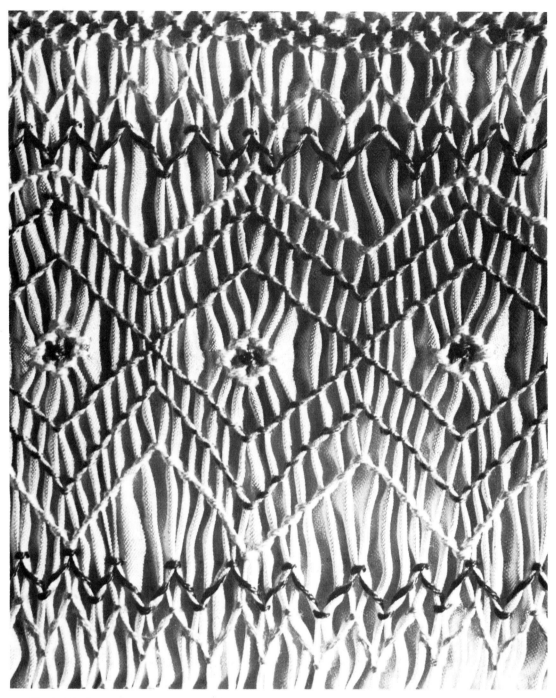

71 *Varying background patterns are formed by the way in which the stitches combine to hold the tubes. Detail taken from a silk wedding dress.* (ANNE ANDREW)

shades of one colour, for example light and medium blue stitchery on a dark blue fabric. Green thread on green fabric with a touch of red would give a successful scheme, whilst purples and pinks worked on a golden yellow could be exciting. Muted or greyed colours such as dusky pink are often easier to combine than brighter colours but, whatever ones are chosen, it is the relative amounts in which they are used which are important. As with other forms of embroidery, a close study of nature will soon suggest perfect colour schemes, especially if the proportion in which each colour appears in the flower, leaf or object being observed is followed within the piece of work. The predominating colour could then be used for the background fabric with the contrasting colours and tones blending for the stitchery.

Working stitches so that they cross over each other can also be a useful device; when two colours are used this allows for more subtle colour blending. Embroider one row of diamond stitch, for example, then work a second row in a different colour over the first one by taking together the tubes missed in the first row (72). There is a tendency, however, in some cases where the 'cross-over' idea is used for the work to become a little tighter and less elastic, so do check this on a sample first.

72 *Cross-over diamond stitch*

THREE-DIMENSIONAL EFFECTS

Because of the geometric nature of smocking it is possible to give greater emphasis to the three-dimensional quality by means of a planned use of colour. There is a tendency to think in terms of one colour being used throughout a row but with a few trials and possible errors some surprising results can be achieved. Work two or three rows of closely spaced wave stitch in a dark thread. Using a lighter tone or possibly white, work another row with the light colour going close above the first row on the upward slope of the wave, then run the thread down behind the tubes to work a lower row on the downward slope. Continue in this manner and a pleated three-dimensional ribbon effect is achieved (73).

A variety of boxes and shapes can be designed in a similar way using different colour tones. It is a help to work the ideas out on graph paper first using coloured pencils or pens and the time spent can be most rewarding. Ethnic designs, tiles, architecture, photographs, books and magazines can all prove to be valuable design sources.

PLANNING A DESIGN

When designing a stitch pattern it is essential to plan the design and work a sample first. The number of tubes in a repeat, as against the number of stitches, can then be carefully counted to ensure accurate placing. For example, a wave which has five stitches up

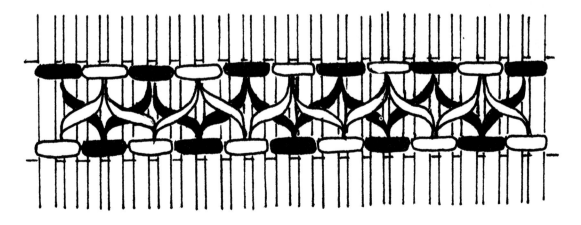

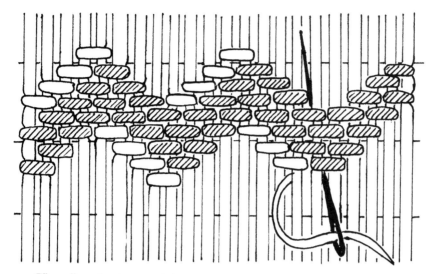

73 *Three-dimensional wave stitch*

and down will be worked over ten tubes for
each repeat. An extra tube should then be
added at each end to complete the design. If
the main pattern design is counted in this
manner the smaller stitch repeats can be fitted
into the number of tubes being used.

It is important to have the largest motif or
design centred in the middle of an area. To
ensure that the pattern will finish at the same
point in the repeat on either side of the panel,
count to the centre tube and mark with a
coloured thread. Find the centre of the actual
design and, starting at this point, smock from
the central tube towards the right-hand side.
Turn the work upside down. Making a neat
join, smock from the centre towards the other
side retaining the continuity of pattern. Once
the sequence is established by means of this
row the smocking can be continued in the
usual way from the beginning of each row.

Seven

Smocking for Fashion Today

GENERAL HINTS ON FASHION SMOCKING

The shape of smocking on a garment is of great importance and needs careful consideration. The depth should always balance and enhance the garment as too much smocking could overwhelm whilst too little could become lost and insignificant. One useful way of testing the balance is to take a drawing or picture of the garment to be made (the one taken from the pattern instruction sheet is ideal) and colour or draw in the proposed area for smocking. A variety of ideas can be tried in this way until the most pleasing one is found.

When smocking is to be used for fashion it is worked before the garment is made up. Generous allowances for seams should be given and then trimmed back during the actual making up. This will prevent any fraying or distortion of the edge of the fabric caused by excessive handling whilst working the design.

The sides of a smocked panel can be neatened by small pin tucks made on the wrong side. The stitching should be as close as possible to the ends of the smocking to cover the start and finishing of the rows. Fine feather stitching can be placed either side of the panel on the front of the fabric if wished.

If smocking is to end where extra elasticity is essential, such as at the waistline, sleeve edge or top of a sundress, a piece of narrow elastic can be loosely stitched using herringbone stitch on the wrong side across the bottom or top of the smocking. This will hold the gathers in place and avoid over stretching through constant wear. In places where texture rather than elasticity is required, such as for a shoulder strap or on a yoke, a fine lining cut to the correct size and shape should be used.

It can be a help, when embroidering two identical panels such as cuffs, collars or bodice fronts, to work them together, stage by stage, as any minor alterations necessary in the design can then be repeated immediately.

ADAPTING COMMERCIAL PATTERNS

Commercial patterns which use smocking may be difficult to find in the style or size required but with careful thought and pre-planning it is possible to adapt many patterns to enable smocking to be included. The following guidelines may help towards this end.

Altering a pattern to give smocking fitted into a simple yoke

Use a simple basic pattern with the desired shaping and fashion details. The following instructions explain how to alter a dress or blouse pattern.

1 Cut out the pattern pieces to be adapted from pattern paper or brown wrapping paper. Mark grain lines, balance marks (used as a guide when connecting seams), also centre front or back (74a).

2 Draw in the yoke line. Mark the balance points on the yoke line and indicate area for added fullness. At least 3 cm ($1\frac{1}{4}$ in.) should be allowed between the start of the gathers and the armhole edge (74b).

3 Cut along the yoke line.

4 Measure the width into which the smocking is to fit.

5 Work a sample of the smocking design using the same weight and type of fabric and thread as you wish to use on the garment to establish the amount of material required for the design.

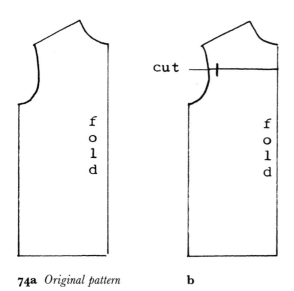

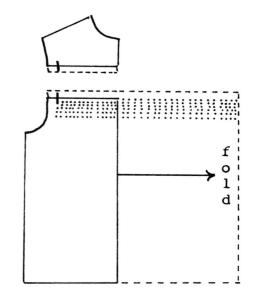

74a *Original pattern*   **b**

c *New pattern pieces*

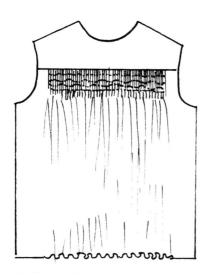

d *Finished front*

6 Calculate the amount to be added for fullness of gathers as in the following example:

If the finished gathered width is equal to 20 cm (8 in.) and the smocking takes up three times the amount of fabric, then the pattern needs to be extended by 40 cm (16 in.). This means that the total width over the area to be smocked will amount to 60 cm (24 in.). Should the smocking take up four times the width then for an area of 20 cm (8 in.) add 60 cm (24 in.), making a total of 80 cm (32 in.).

7 Extend the lower pattern piece the required amount.

8 Add seam allowances at the bottom of the yoke and the top of the lower section. Indicate grain lines and balance marks *(74c)*.

9 Use the new pattern pieces to cut out the fabric.

Fullness can be added in other areas in a similar manner. Figure 75 shows how a long sleeve could be adapted.

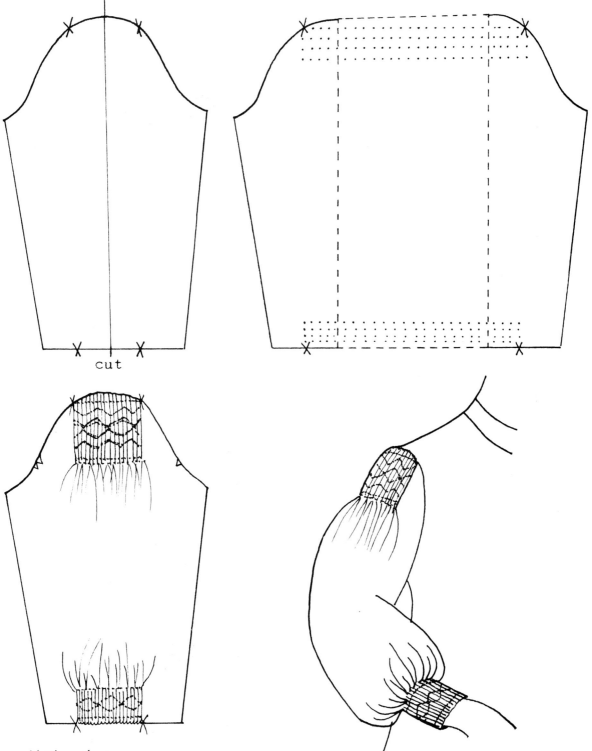

cut

75 *Adapting a sleeve*

PEASANT-STYLE BLOUSE

Nothing could be simpler or more effective than a smocked, peasant-style blouse. A version made in silk would look lovely for the evening whilst cotton, wool mixture or a fine wool jersey could be used to make a tunic style to be worn with a skirt or over trousers.

The blouse shown in colour plate 7 is made from white lawn with the smocking worked over 6 mm ($\frac{1}{4}$ in.) dots using four tones of reddish gold and two tones of greenish beige silk buttonhole twist. The design is made up of cable, cross-over diamond in two tones, trellis and wave stitches.

To make a similar garment use a basic raglan sleeve blouse pattern for the armhole curves. Following the layout in figure 77, extend the pattern by the required amount. The front is cut 2.5 cm (1 in.) shorter than the back.

76 *Detail of peasant blouse.* (JEAN HODGES. PHOTO: PETER DOWNS)

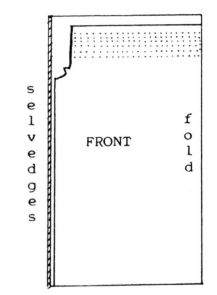

77a and **b** *Extending a basic blouse pattern*

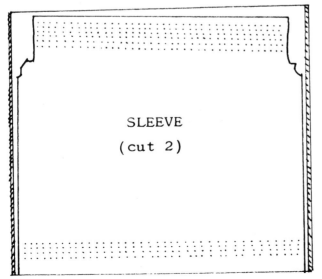

c *The top of the sleeve pattern slopes to make the front edge 2.5 cm (1 in.) shorter than the back*

Assess the quantity of fabric by allowing twice the garment length plus twice the sleeve length. The width will depend on the stitch design and weight of fabric chosen. The finer the fabric the more fullness will be required whereas a thick, heavier fabric will take less and the dots will need to be spaced further apart.

Prepare the fabric by pre-shrinking, pressing and removing the selvedges. Check that the warp and weft threads are at right angles and cut the garment out.

Note that the neck is cut on the straight of grain as it is the choice of stitches which will cause the yoke to curve. If the pattern to be used has a curved neckline and the shape of the curve is being retained, slash the dots as shown in figure 40.

Mark the centre of each piece and apply the necessary rows of dots – 14 to 18 rows for the neckline and eight to ten rows on each cuff. To work out the number of dots required for a design, count the number of tubes and then add an extra dot. A tube is the space between two dots.

Match the dots carefully at the row endings to make certain the seams will run through the dots. This ensures that when the gathering is pulled up the seam will come at the bottom of the tube and remain invisible. Stitch the shoulder seams. Trim the seam allowance back to 1 cm ($\frac{3}{8}$ in.) and neaten by oversewing the edges together.

If the smocked area is to end with a ruffle, a narrow rolled hem is made before drawing up the gathering threads. The first row of dots is placed approximately 4 cm ($1\frac{1}{2}$ in.) down from the hem.

All the shoulder seams can be joined and then the fabric gathered and pulled up into a tube if the neckline is wide enough not to need an opening. When inserting the gathering threads to form this tube, each pair of threads should start and finish in a different place so that they do not run vertically under each other. This will help to keep the gathers smooth and even for smocking. It will be

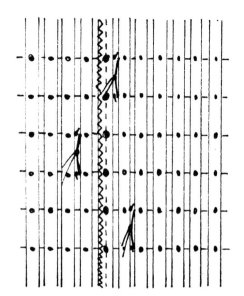

78 *Fabric seamed with the gathering threads staggered so that each pair of threads starts and finishes in a different place*

found easier if, on this occasion, each pair of drawn up threads is knotted together instead of being twisted round a pin which could get in the way of the embroidery.

To create a suitable smocking design the stitches nearest the neck will need to be firm and close to give most control to the gathers. Gradually the pattern can become more decorative and open. The last set of rows should have deep waves or points to give the most stretch and allow the tubes to fan out.

Begin the smocking at one of the back seams, ignoring the first gathering thread. Several rows of cable stitch can be worked on the back of the top rows to keep the ruffle from rolling forward.

Using a variation of the main design, gather and smock the sleeves. These can be worked flat and then the seams joined, matching each row of smocking. The sleeve edge is neatened by means of a small rolled hem. Complete the garment according to the pattern instructions.

79 *Rectangles of fabric smocked and cut to shape to add textural interest to the yoke and cuffs of a polyester blouse. The narrow piping gives a neat finish.* (CHRIS SPICE)

SHAPED SMOCKING

When smocking is to be fitted into a neckline or armhole it is possible to cut the smocking dots to the required shape before they are applied but this can cause certain difficulties, especially in maintaining the flow and stitch design. It is much easier and avoids unnecessary distortion if the smocking is worked as a straight panel and then cut to shape in the following manner.

Smock the fabric on the straight grain to the required depth and to a width equivalent to the widest measurement of the pattern piece. Remove all but the first and last gathering threads and pin the smocking out to shape on an ironing board or other suitable surface. Place the paper pattern on the embroidery taking care to match the centre of the pattern to the centre tube for its entire length. Pin in position and tack around the cutting line. Remove the pattern piece and machine stitch just within the seam

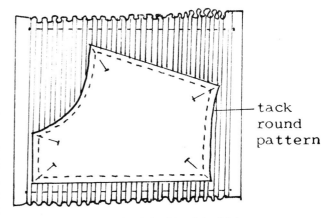

80 *Pattern pinned to the right side of the fabric*

65

allowance. The embroidery can now be cut out and made up like any other piece of fabric without fear of the work unravelling.

With this principle in mind, many new ideas and areas come within the scope of the embroiderer. Rectangles of white polyester fabric, smocked with crochet cotton over 6 mm ($\frac{1}{4}$ in.) dots, were cut to shape and used to make the yokes and cuffs of a classic blouse (79). Narrow piping cord completes the highly textural design. Shaped collars, cuffs, yokes and pockets can all be enhanced with smocking and a variety of textures obtained by altering the direction of the tubes so that they run horizontally as well as vertically.

HORIZONTAL SMOCKING

Placing smocking horizontally can add yet another dimension and is well worth considering as the light will run across rather than down the gathers, thus giving an entirely different effect. It also has the added advantage of the tubes being included into the side seams. This allows freedom for any shaping required in the unsmocked areas to be added by means of darts rather than the usual fullness of gathers. Silk used in this way with added beads and surface stitchery could produce an exciting and exclusive outfit. Fabric always drapes better when cut with the warp (long) threads running vertically so remember, if smocking in this way, that the pattern pieces will need to be turned and cut with the grain line on the pattern running across the fabric (81b).

Place the pattern on the fabric allowing for the extra material required for smocking. Tack round on the cutting line to indicate the shape where there will be no smocking. Cut out slightly larger to avoid fraying and distortion caused by excessive handling whilst working on the gathers. After completing the smocking, replace the pattern piece and machine stitch just inside the cutting line of the smocked area. Cut out and finish according to the pattern instructions.

An eye catching feature showing textural contrast could be emphasized by smocking just one shoulder or area in this manner. A small pin tuck placed on the back as described on page 59 will form a neat, unobtrusive finish where the smocking runs into an unsmocked area.

Horizontally worked bodice fronts have been inserted into the simple, long sleeved, cream wool dress (82). The pattern is made up

81a *Normal pattern placing*

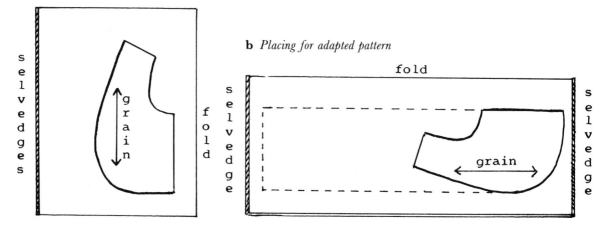

b *Placing for adapted pattern*

82 *The horizontal placing of the smocking on the bodice of a wool dress causes the light to run across the tubes and give added depth to the design.* (JEAN HODGES)

of wave, trellis, satin and cross-over diamond stitch and worked in shades of pink and brown silk buttonhole twist over 6 mm ($\frac{1}{4}$ in.) dots. In the large diamond-shaped area, where there is no stitching, the tubes have been held on the back with a row of cable stitch. Narrow cotton lace has been applied at the edge of the insertion to complete the design.

Where two areas of smocking which reflect each other are being used in close proximity such as on the bodice front, it is necessary to check the design and colour balance carefully. This can be done quite easily by holding a sample piece at right angles against a mirror and seeing its reflection. You will then see how the stitch patterns and colours will relate to each other. If the sample looks wrong one way, turn it upside down and try it again. Sections can be pinned out of the way or other pieces added, and colours or stitch patterns changed around, until the result is pleasing.

INSERTIONS

Smocked insertions can be an effective yet simple way of adding a decorative or textural panel to a garment. The panel can be worked in a contrast or the same fabric as the main part of the garment. A contrast fabric is especially useful when working in 'difficult' fabrics such as velvet, heavy wools or bouclé where the gathering could create problems or too much bulk. Matt fabrics can be combined with silky ones; smooth with textured or light with heavy to give a creative and exclusive finish. Inserts have the advantage that they can be added without altering the main style or drape of a garment. They are worked on the straight but can be manipulated into curves and can therefore be placed almost anywhere – on the bodice, skirt or sleeves, running either vertically or horizontally. The following instructions and diagrams show how to place the insertion across a bodice front, but they apply equally to any other placing.

1 Draw lines on the pattern pieces to indicate where the smocked insert will be placed.

2 Cut the fabric for smocking, allowing at least 2.5 cm (1 in.) extra above and below the area to be smocked.

3 Allowing an extra gathering thread above and below the actual stitching, work the smocking insert. Remove all but the top and bottom gathering threads which are left loosely in place to help with making up. Test the finished piece for size against the marked area of the pattern.

83a *Original pattern*

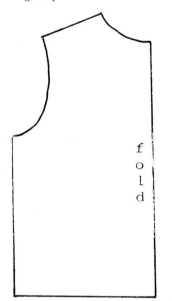

b *New pattern for yoke and main section*

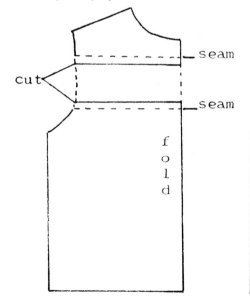

c *Insertion stitched in place*

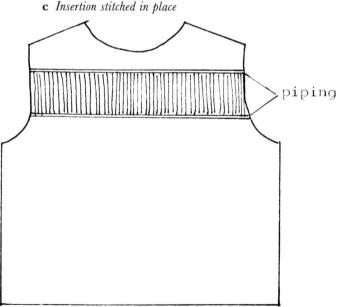

68

4 Cut the paper pattern apart where the smocking is to be inserted, making allowances for the seams.

5 Cut out the fabric using these adapted pattern pieces.

6 Place the smocking on the garment piece with the right sides together. Distribute the gathers evenly and tack in place.

7 Stitch along the seam line. Trim away any excess fabric on the insert and neaten the raw edges by oversewing or a zigzag stitch.

8 Complete the garment according to the pattern instructions.

To prevent the bulk from the smocking puckering the garment a narrow piping can be inserted:

1 Using the same or contrasting fabric cut two pieces of piping (see page 112) the width of the pattern where the insert is to be placed.

2 Pin the piping along the top and bottom of the insert on the first and last gathering thread. The piping cord should be towards the inside of the insert.

3 Distribute the pleats evenly and tack close to the piping cord.

4 Place the smocking and piping on the garment with right sides together. Stitch close to the ridge of the piping cord. Trim away the excess fabric. Neaten the raw edges.

5 Repeat on the other edge of the insert.

Lace, ribbon trim or surface embroidery could be used in place of the piping to give a neat finish.

When a smocked section needs to be firmly controlled use the cut-out piece of the pattern as a guide, adding 1.5 cm ($\frac{5}{8}$ in.) seam allowances, and cut a lining to back the smocking. After inserting the panel and making up the garment turn all the seam allowances of the lining section to the wrong side. Tack and press. Pin and tack the lining to the back of the smocked area, wrong sides together, and stitch in place by hand.

Insertions can also be used on ready-made garments following the guidelines given.

Skirts and sleeves are particularly suitable and would require the minimum of alteration. For accurate placing, measure up from the hemline when inserting a panel into a skirt.

CHILDREN'S WEAR

Smocking has always been popular for use in children's clothing. Christening robes, babies' bonnets, dresses or romper suits, party dresses and pinafores can all include areas of smocking although an even wider application is possible for older children's clothing. The fact that a child's lifestyle has changed from the Victorian days when smocking was so popular does not mean that it is no longer appropriate for everyday wear. Needlecord, viyella, calico and polyester/cotton which are practical, hardwearing and easy to launder can be used for a variety of styles.

Panels of honeycomb smocking can be set vertically into a quilted or plain jacket to allow for growth and give extra elasticity and movement. Insertions can be used in many ways to add interest and style without making the garment too fussy: on the front of a dress or the bib of dungarees, to form the waistband of a skirt or trousers, as well as for a pretty blouse or dress.

WEDDING DRESS AND CORONET

The richness of triple honeycomb stitch on gleaming white satin with the added mother-of-pearl effect created by sprayed fabric paint were the inspiration for the wedding dress and coronet in colour plate 5. This was brought about by a chance experiment where, as so often happens, the results were quite unexpected (see page 102). It is impossible to capture the true effect in a still photograph as it is only by movement that the elusive, opalescent quality can be fully appreciated.

The dress of organza over satin was designed on very simple, classic lines so as not to detract from the richness of the smocking. The satin cuffs were smocked using triple

84 *Ideas for using smocking on outdoor garments.*
(PAULINE MACKENZIE)

85 *Adding texture with vertical and horizontally placed smocking.* (PAULINE MACKENZIE)

86 *Suggestions for evening wear.* (PAULINE MACKENZIE)

7 *Peasant blouse worked in six tones of silk buttonhole twist on cotton lawn by Jean Hodges for Elizabeth Hodges. (Photo: Mike Farmer)*

8 *The neckline of this polyester/cotton baby dress is cut on the straight of the grain with smocking used to create the curve. Bullion knot rosebuds give an attractive finish to the simple design. Made by Joy Hopkyn-Rees.*

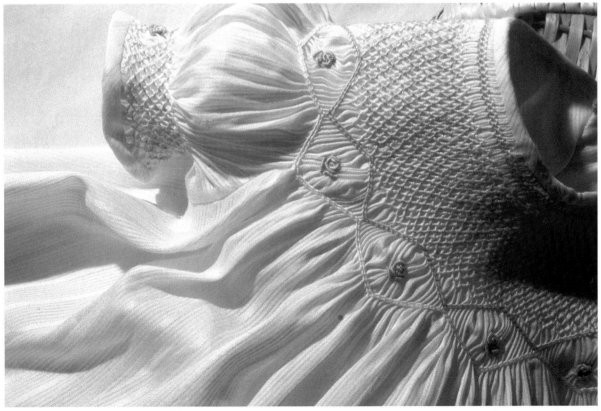

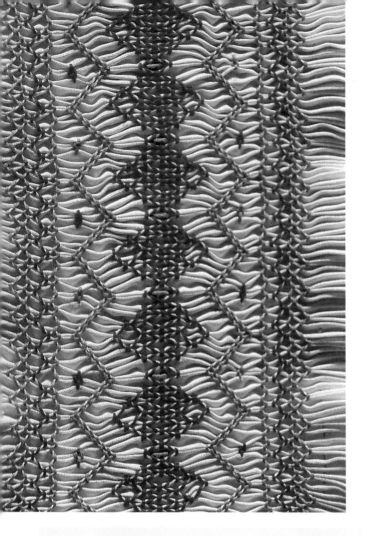

9 Here Jean Hodges has used cable, diamond and wave stitch with small flowerettes for extra impact. 'The horizontally placed tubes help to catch the light.'

10 A combination of reverse smocking, quilting and hand stitching have been used on these panne velvet, three-dimensional pigeons. Made by Jill Friend.

11 *French knots and beads nestle into a*
   background of reverse smocking to form the
   base of a richly decorated silk box.
   From the Embroiderers' Guild Collection.

12 *Smocked tussah silk inserted into a velvet
cushion.
Made by Jean Hodges.*

87 *Tucks and smocking could combine on silk.*
(PAULINE MACKENZIE)

88 *Ideas for children's clothing.* (PAULINE MACKENZIE)

89 *Triple honeycomb-smocked and fabric-sprayed satin incorporated into a wedding dress. See colour plate 5.* (JEAN HODGES. PHOTO: PETER DOWNS)

honeycomb stitch over 1.25 cm ($\frac{1}{2}$ in.) dots, sprayed and faced with fine cotton lawn which had been cut to shape. The dress was made up to be complete without the smocked yoke. The back and front yoke pieces were smocked as rectangles, sprayed with fabric paint, cut to shape and mounted onto a lawn backing and then the shoulder seams were stitched. The backing was used to hold the slightly stretched smocking in place as well as to form a thin lining. The neckline was finished by means of a bias strip on the wrong side with slip stitches going through both the lining and the smocking. The back opening was neatened, button loops worked and small satin-covered buttons attached. The completed inset was then slip stitched to the neck

facing of the dress and the bottom edge of the yoke was neatened by oversewing to the bottom of the facing. A row of feather stitching was added about 2.5 cm (1 in.) below the smocking to complete the design.

The coronet was honeycomb-smocked, sprayed and embellished with drop pearls, small beads and French knots, then mounted over a wide Alice band.

ACCESSORIES

For many years babies' bonnets have displayed some very fine smocking and this tradition still continues. However, hats in general can be the subject for imaginative and creative use of the technique. Most large department stores sell simple hat forms which can be used as the basis for a smocked 'creation', ranging from the practical to the purely frivolous. A simple shape worked in wool would keep the head warm whilst ruched and smocked silk or organza could be turned into a most romantic bridal or Ascot hat.

A piece of watered taffeta was worked in triple honeycomb stitch and then moulded and stitched onto a pre-formed shape to create an attractive and unusual bridesmaid's hat as shown in figure 90. A small spray of fresh or artificial flowers can be added at the side.

Bags and purses of all shapes and sizes have proved a challenging yet ideal surface for adornment by the embroiderer. This also holds true for smocking, which can be combined with leathers, suede, silks or contrasting firm fabrics for attractive day or evening bags. The contrasting fabric can be used for the binding, piping, gussets and handles according to the design and type of bag being considered.

Honeycomb stitch was used to decorate the flap of the black silk evening bag shown in figure 91. A decorative bead was added when taking the second stitch over the tubes. The panel, set into straight strips of silk fabric, is mounted onto wadding backed with pelmet

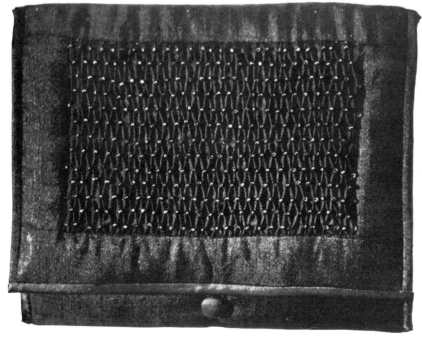

90 *Triple honeycomb smocking on watered taffeta moulded to form an attractive bridesmaid's cap.* (MAUREEN DEDMAN)

91 *Black silk clutch bag. The decorative je beads were added when taking the second stitch over the tubes.* (ANNE ANDREW)

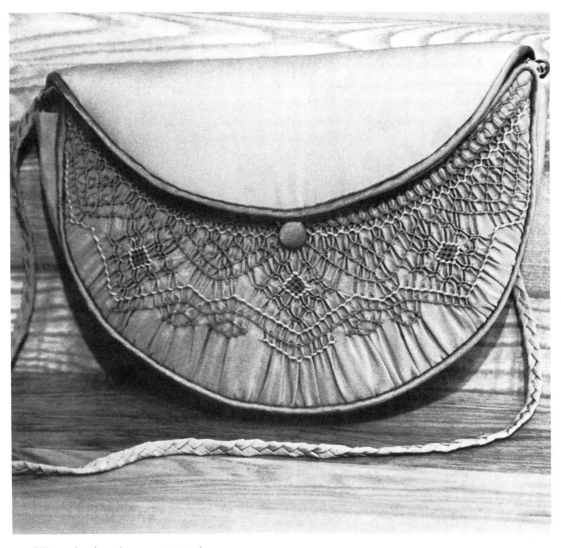

92 *Silk evening bag.* (ANNE ANDREW)

vilene to give a firm finish. The clutch bag is lined with silk, edged with a bias cut binding and fastened by means of a covered button and loop.

A rectangle of smocked fabric can be manipulated into a variety of curves to create imaginatively shaped day and evening bags. Binding or fabric-covered piping cord, a fastening and a suitable handle can then be added to complete the bag.

A versatile tote bag can be made by smocking a piece of hessian, denim or furnishing fabric using heavy thread. Wooden beads or tassels could be added and then a calico or similar fabric lining inserted. Plastic sheeting can be used to line the bag for the beach.

Belts and cummerbunds of various shapes, sizes and fabrics can also be enhanced with areas of smocking adding further embellishment if required.

93 *The simplicity of cable, chain and honeycomb stitch combine to create the textural effect on the flap of a clutch bag.* (KARIN TOLSON)

FRILLS AND RUFFLES

Narrow, delicate frills look charming down the front of a dress or blouse, round a cuff or neckline, down sleeves or at the hem of a skirt. Quickly and simply made frills can add a touch of glamour to any outfit and are especially useful to brighten up a simple ready-made garment and add an exclusive look. They can also be placed down the front of a man's evening shirt. A 6 cm ($2\frac{1}{2}$ in.) wide strip can be gathered and decorated with two or three rows of honeycomb, surface honeycomb or diamond stitch outlined with cable or wave stitch. The edges can be finished by means of a rolled hem, buttonhole stitching or embroidered on an automatic sewing machine using a matching or contrast thread. After neatening the narrow edges the frill can be slip stitched in place. A more complicated design can, of course, be used but sometimes the simplest stitches can be the most effective. Silk, satin, organza or lawn would all look delightful and the edges could be finished with a narrow lace for an added air of luxury.

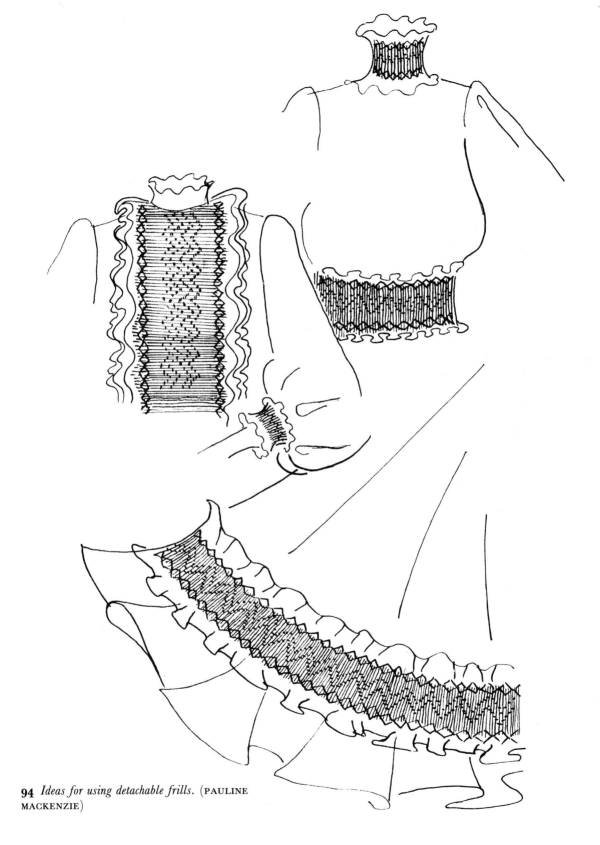

94 *Ideas for using detachable frills.* (PAULINE
MACKENZIE)

Eight

Practical Ideas for the Home

Smocking can be used both effectively and imaginatively in many ways around the home. Cushions, curtains, valances (gathered pelmets) and ties, bed valances, lampshades, boxes, wall hangings and panels can all successfully include smocking within their design.

CUSHIONS

Cushions make an ideal background for experimentation and offer the opportunity to combine a variety of techniques. Here the effect required is decorative and textural in contrast to the style and shaping necessary for fashion. Obviously some form of cleaning will be needed but the problems are not as great and a wider range of fabrics can be considered, providing they are firm enough and suitable for the amount of wear the cushion will receive. Cushions play a vital role in the decorative scheme of a room and the inclusion of smocking can give extra impact. The stitching can be in a variety of tonal values for a textural effect or in a sharp contrast to bring life to a scheme.

A smocked panel can be inserted into a cushion cover so that it is framed by the fabric from which the rest of the cover is made. This is done before making up the cover. Since elasticity is not an important factor it is possible to build up dense stitch designs using a variety of threads with the possible addition of extra surface embroidery or beads.

Cream tussah silk, gathered at 6 mm ($\frac{1}{4}$ in.) intervals and smocked with silk buttonhole twist has been inserted into green furnishing velvet in the cushion shown in figure 95. A row of twisted chain stitch frames the insert to complete the design.

To work a cushion in this manner, choose a toning or contrast-coloured fabric and threads and work a panel to the required size allowing 1.25 cm ($\frac{1}{2}$ in.) for turnings.

1 Measure the slightly stretched insert accurately. Draw the exact size using tailor's chalk, or tack with contrast tacking cotton onto the right side of the fabric which is to form the surround, making sure the panel is centrally positioned.

2 Draw a second line 1.25 cm ($\frac{1}{2}$ in.) inside the first line to create a seam allowance. Cut the shape out following the inner line. To reinforce the corners stitch 2.5 cm (1 in.) either side of the corners on the seam line.

3 Snip diagonally into the corners of the seam allowance up to the stitched line. Turn the 1.25 cm ($\frac{1}{2}$ in.) seam allowance to the wrong side and tack in place.

4 Mark the centre and quarters of both the smocking and the surround where the panel is being inserted.

5 Carefully position the insert under the hole, matching the marks and pin in place making sure the gathers are evenly spaced. Slip stitch the panel in place.

The edge of the smocked panel can be decorated with a fine twisted cord or couched thread to give a neat finish. The cushion cover is then made up in the usual manner.

LAMPSHADES

Lampshades play an important role in a furnishing scheme and as well as being functional they should also be decorative. For this reason smocking is an ideal technique for use in either a simple or a more complicated form. Silk chiffon worked in a combination of smocking and soft pleating can be restful and delicate whilst a honeycomb-smocked shade using a heavier fabric with added beads, fringing or tassels can be quite dramatic. The

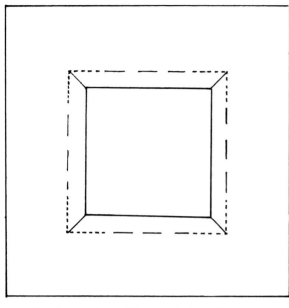

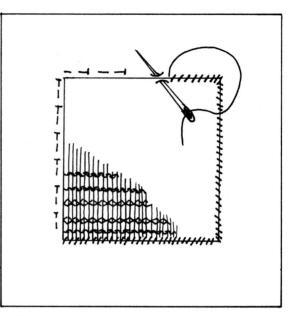

96a *Cut out shape following the inner line*

b *Pin smocked panel behind frame and slip stitch in place*

smocking can be worked in bands to go round the top of a tiffany type shade; used as insertions combined with plain panels or, in a completely free, random manner covering the whole shade. Reference should be made to a book on lampshade-making for the general instructions but the following guidelines apply when working smocking for this purpose.

1 The width of the fabric needed should be assessed over the widest part of the shade to be covered by the smocking.

2 Carefully join all the seams, by hand or machine, to form a tube, trimming the seams back to 6 mm ($\frac{1}{4}$ in.), and gather as described on page 64. If using insertions, refer to page 68.

3 Extra care should be taken when starting and finishing threads to make them as neat and invisible as possible so that they do not show when the light is on. The light from the lamp will also show up the density of the tubes and the patterns they form where they are pulled together, as well as the stitchery; therefore, having worked a sample, hold it up

to a naked bulb to judge the overall effect and make any necessary design adjustments.

4 When all the smocking is complete the work should be steamed and the gathering threads removed except for those at the top and the bottom. These threads are slackened and used to hold the gathers evenly whilst fitting the fabric over the frame. Once the cover is stitched onto the frame any excess fabric can be trimmed away and the shade completed.

CURTAINS AND TIE-BACKS

Bands of straight or pointed smocking can be worked to hold the gathers and add a textural finish to a curtain heading or valance with smocked tie-backs to complete the attractive effect. To give a crisp look, the smocking on the tie-backs can be applied to pelmet vilene or buckram which will act as interfacing and hold the work firmly. The tie-backs are then lined using a matching fabric and a narrow piping inserted round the edge to give a neat finish. Nets can also have a delicate heading added by means of simple smocking and

95 *A velvet cushion with an insert of tussah silk smocked in silk buttonhole twist. The stitches used are outline, cable, diamond, feather and satin stitch with twisted chain stitch to frame the insert.* (JEAN HODGES)

again, tie-backs can be created from a strip of smocking in the form of a frill with narrow rolled hems to neaten the edges.

An enchantingly romantic effect can be achieved by using smocking to control the gathers on the drapery around a baby's crib or basket. A fine lawn, voile or robia voile (satin-striped voile) would look delightful worked in pastel shades with the addition of lace and matching ribbons. A similar theme could be used on a cot quilt or pillow.

97 *Ideas for a lampshade, mirror and photograph frames.* (PAULINE MACKENZIE)

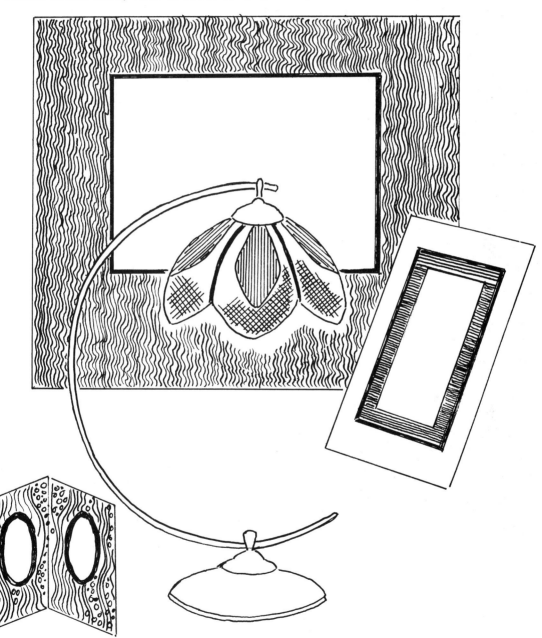

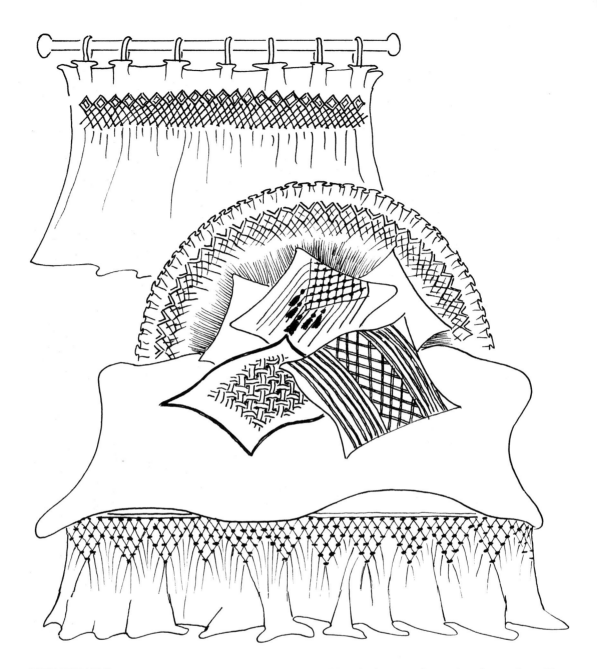

BEDHEADS

A bedroom can take on a completely new look by the use of smocking on a simply shaped bedhead. The effect can be light and feminine by combining a fine fabric, delicate stitchery and lace, or luxurious by using a rich-looking fabric such as velvet or satin and honeycomb stitch with the possible addition of silk or gold tassels.

98 *Ideas for incorporating various forms of smocking into furnishing.* (PAULINE MACKENZIE)

Fabric boxes, mirror and photograph frames can also include all forms of smocking to give a lively and individual finish. In fact, smocking proves to be an increasingly versatile form of embroidery once its wider application is fully appreciated.

84

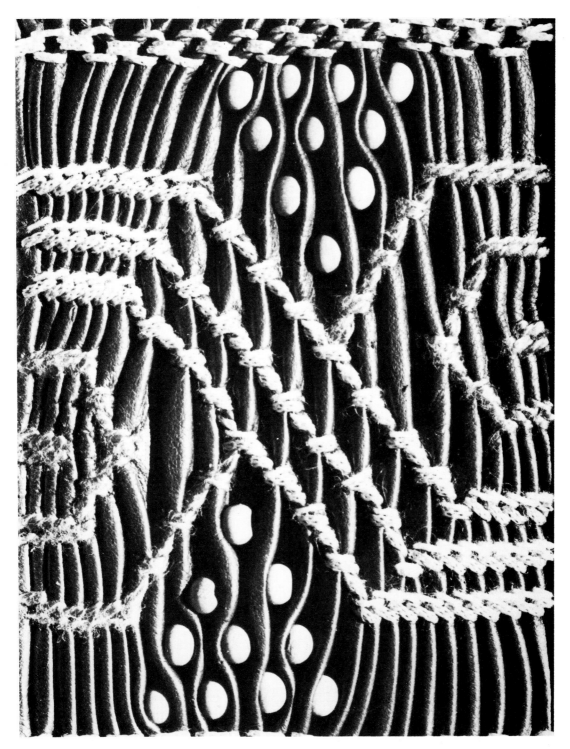

99 *A sample showing fine leather smocked in wool and sylko perlé with added beads.* (ANNE ANDREW)

Nine

Free Smocking

Gather up a piece of soft fabric and push it in various directions to see how the tubes can move and ripple, making ever-changing patterns and shapes. The shapes created may well suggest natural forms such as waterfalls, a rippling stream, tree bark, wood grain, shifting sand or the more rigid lines used in architecture. If a conventional piece of smocking is gently stretched and viewed from the back it is easy to let the imagination roam and visualize endless possibilities. It is because of this ability to manipulate smocking so easily and effectively that the technique can now be exploited and used to advantage in ways which have not been considered in the past.

FABRICS AND METHODS
New fabrics are constantly appearing in the shops, so be prepared to experiment. Interesting effects can be obtained with the most unconventional fabric. The play of light on the ripples and folds of gathered organza, shot silk or heavy satin can be exploited in many exciting ways for hangings, panels or three-dimensional objects. Panne velvet has been used for the three-dimensional pigeons (100). The breasts are worked in reverse smocking with uneven honeycomb holding the gathers on the wrong side. Also included are hand quilting on the wings and tail with free Cretan stitch around the head and neck.

Reverse smocking can open up new ideas. The tubes are held by smocking stitches on the back leaving the right side free for further development. The technique has the same gathering preparation as traditional smocking except that the fabric is picked up above

100 *Reverse smocking with uneven honeycomb stitch holding the panne velvet on the wrong side has been used for the three-dimensional pigeons. Also included are hand quilting on the wings and tails with free Cretan stitch around the neck and head.* (JILL FRIEND)

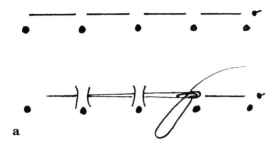

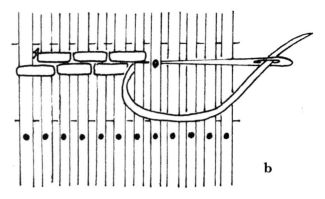

101a *Picking up fabric for reverse smocking*
b *Wrong side of fabric*

the dots instead of on them (*101a*). Having secured the gathering threads, hold the tubes in place by rows of smocking, using the appropriate weight and colour of thread on the wrong side. The stitching is worked along the actual line of dots (*101b*). Avoid picking up too much fabric when working on the back as the stitches may be inclined to show through to the front. Cable stitch will produce firmly controlled gathers whilst honeycomb stitch allows greater elasticity. Experimentation with the holding stitches on the back can produce varied results on the right side. This method of holding the tubes is also used when working motifs on the front, leaving areas unsmocked as described on page 50.

The regular lines of straight smocking inspired the panel Summer Grasses (*104*). The effect was achieved by reverse smocking a piece of calico which was then applied to a calico background. The gathers were manipulated and held in place by straight surface stitches using a variety of threads and ribbons to give added highlights and contrast of texture. Additional pieces of freely smocked stockinette were then manipulated and applied to the surface to indicate clumps of cow parsley.

In contrast, rows of outline stitch worked on the reverse of green silk gave a controlled rippling appearance suggesting the movement of long grass (*105*). Iron-on vilene was applied to the back of yellow silk to form the individual petals of the buttercups which are held in place by French knots. French knots and their variants also nestle amongst the gathers.

A partially destroyed wasps' nest inspired the experimental work shown in figure *106*. A piece of grey cotton jersey was gathered up and, in order to obtain the different effects, both surface and reverse smocking were used. In certain areas the gathering stitches remain to help the structure of the rippled movement in the sample. The applied rosette shape was achieved by gathering a rectangular piece of satin. This was smocked and formed into a circle before being attached. Surface stitches were added afterwards.

DESIGN SOURCES
As compared with traditional smocking, which is more or less restricted to geometric patterns, the modern use of the technique can give unrestricted freedom of expression. Since smocked fabric can be moulded and draped to give a variety of effects, a study of nature, always a source of inspiration to any artist, will prove most rewarding.

Water cascading over rocks makes an ideal subject. Straight tubes could be held in place by reverse and surface smocking for the actual waterfall with, possibly, ruched fabrics, appliqué or surface stitchery worked by hand or machine for the foam and spray. The idea

87

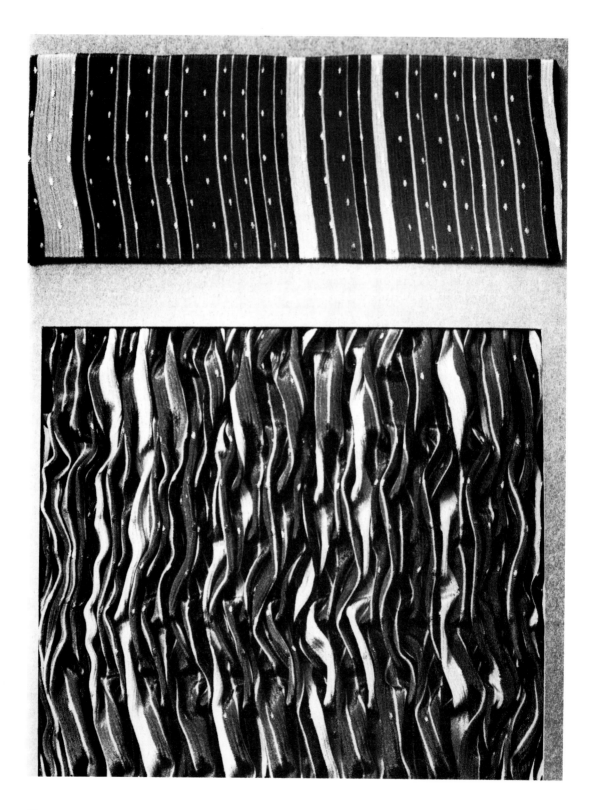

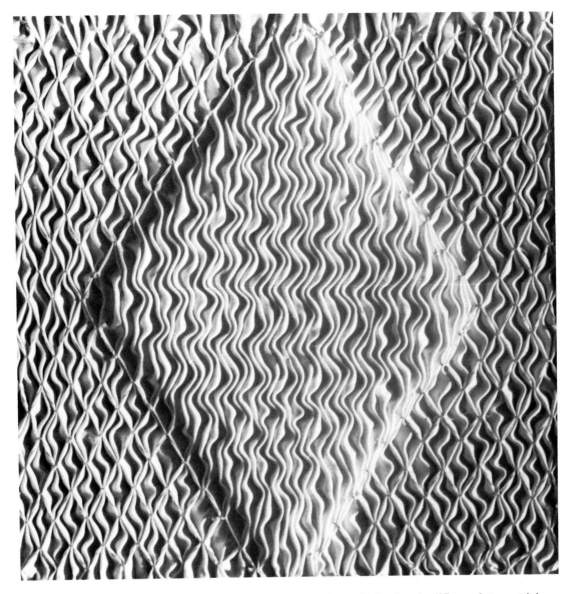

103 *A sample showing the difference between triple honeycomb worked on the back of the fabric in the central diamond shape and on the front for the surround.* (JEAN HODGES)

102 *Random herringbone stitch worked on the back of a striped fabric.* (PATRICIA BROUGHALL)

104 *Buttercup Field: outline stitch worked on the reverse of green silk with added appliqué and French knots.* (VAL PALMER)

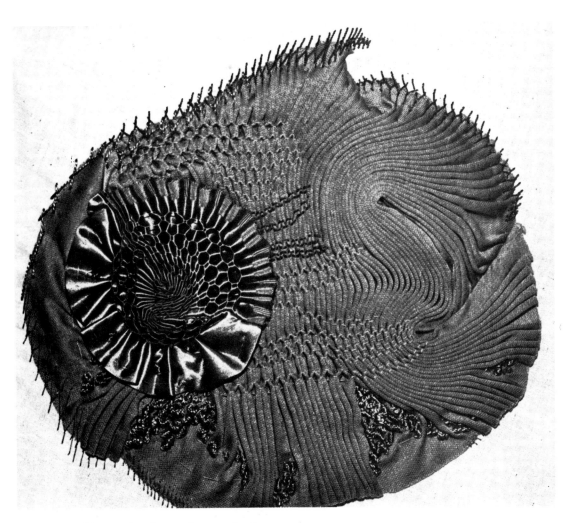

105 *Wasp's Nest: gathered cotton jersey and satin using reverse and surface smocking with added surface stitchery.* (ROS CHILCOT. PHOTO: ANDREW HODGES)

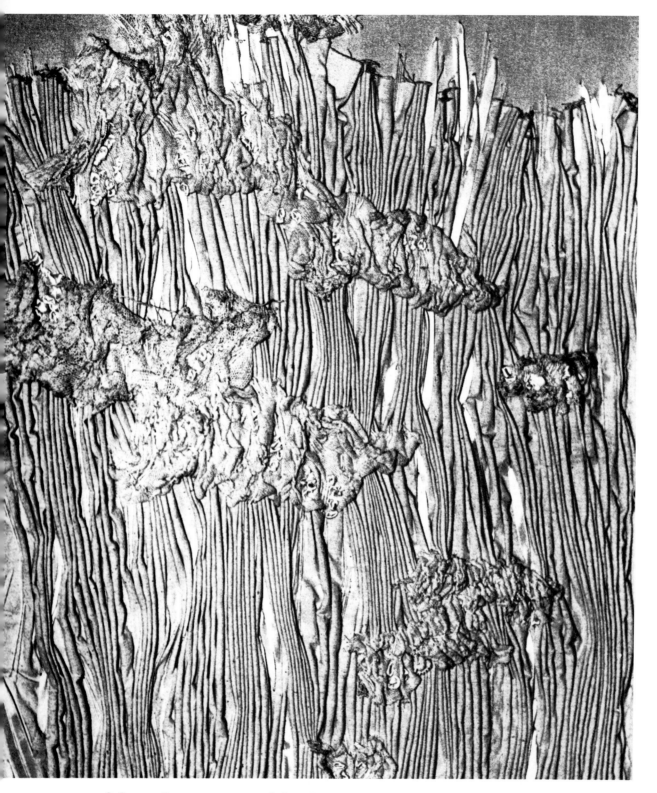

106 *Summer Grasses: a reverse-smocked panel approximately 80 cm × 50 cm (31 in. × 19 in.). Pieces of freely smocked stockinette were manipulated and applied to the surface to indicate clumps of cow parsley.* (JEAN LITTLEJOHN. PHOTO: ANDREW HODGES)

107 *Random-smocked organza over deep tubes was manipulated onto silver kid with added surface stitchery, rouleau cords, fringing and gathered and fringed suede.* (CYNTHIA SHERWOOD)

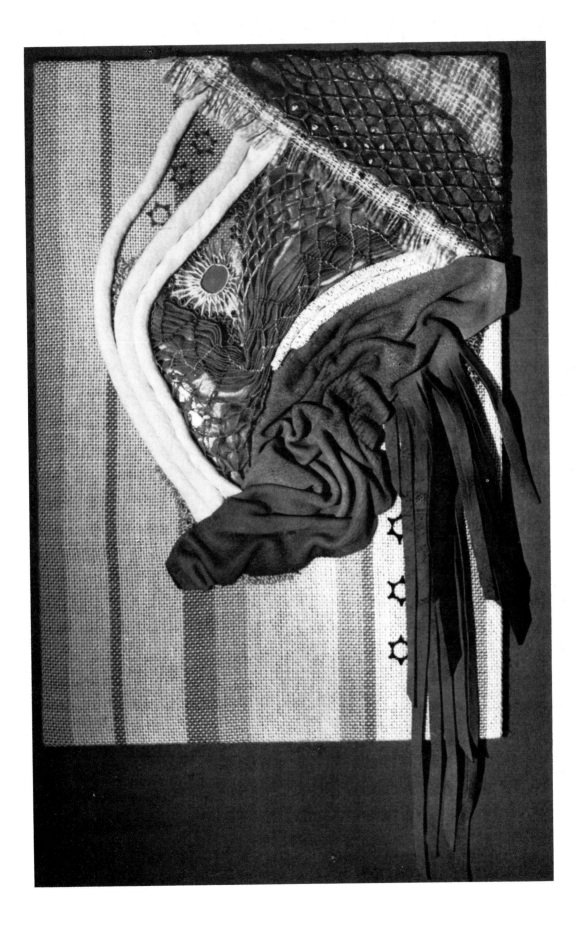

could work equally well for a panel or three-dimensional object. When depicting water it helps to have some form of light, either direct or reflected, to add to the illusion. This can be a spotlight directed onto the work from a suitable angle; or natural light from a window or reflected by a mirror. A Victorian mirror was chosen as the ideal background for the waterfall panel (*108*). Not only does the mirror reflect the light through the folds in the fabric but the shelf at the bottom gives a firm base to allow the design to be built up using polystyrene blocks at the side. A wide selection of fine fabrics including plastic sheeting was surface smocked with areas cut away to help the reflection from the mirror. Beads, ribbons, cords, wools, shisha glass and surface embroidery have all been added to give atmosphere to the rocks and undergrowth with machine-embroidered organza for the detached leaves.

109 *Lampshade based on a waterfall design. Freely smocked silk chiffon has been applied to a chiffon covered frame. Gathering threads have been retained to give emphasis to the rocks. Reverse smocked opalescent fabric with added beads gives the feeling of movement to the water whilst wisps of wool form the spray.* (SHIELA DE KRETZER)

110 *Detail of the waterfall lampshade.* (SHIELA DE KRETZER)

108 *Waterfall: surface smocking, beads, ribbons, cords, wools and shisha glass with added hand and machine embroidery have been mounted onto a Victorian mirror.* (ROS CHILCOT)

111 *Seashore: the movement of the waves comes from shot blue/yellow organza which was reverse smocked with close cable stitch at the horizon, gradually becoming more widely spaced towards the foreground. Detached loop stitches are added to the waves with massed French knots for the sand. Detached buttonhole and free Cretan stitch are used for the birds.* (ANNA DIAMOND)

112 *Reverse-smocked calico has been used for the stalk and gills of the three-dimensional toadstool with suede for the cap and canvas work for the base.* (CAROLE TOMPKINS)

An exciting and unusual lampshade could also be made from this design source. A firm, opaque fabric could be used for the main part of the shade with areas of Italian quilting, trapunto or stitchery to suggest a rocky outcrop. Organza or similarly sheer fabric smocked, draped and inserted to form the waterfall would allow the light to shine through to bring the design to life.

Most forms of fungus with their interesting textural quality make ideal sources of inspiration. They can be translated in a wide range of fabrics and techniques and incorporated into many different projects. The stalk and underside of the toadstool (*112*) have been worked in reverse smocking using one rectangle of calico. The stem area is held by cable stitch whilst the underside of the cap is worked in surface honeycomb stitch to give elasticity and allow for shaping. Peat brown Indian ink brushed over the tubes before removing the gathering threads adds colour to the underside. Cotton reels support the stem whilst terylene wadding fills the suede leather cap. The toadstool is attached to a base worked in velvet stitch and French knots over coarse plastic canvas.

Patches of scrunchy French knots and beads nestling within the folds of reverse smocking can be used to interpret rubbings taken from wood grain whilst both surface and reverse smocking on hessian would be suitable for the roughness of tree bark. Areas

113 *Tree bark inspired the inside of this richly decorated silk box. French knots and beads nestle within the reverse smocked tubes.* (THE EMBROIDERERS' GUILD COLLECTION)

of cutwork and needleweaving with a background of leather or other suitable fabric could suggest gnarling and wood knots. Sections can be padded and shaped to give an added dimension.

A close study of various types of shells will soon show that they are also ideally suited for interpretation by means of this technique. Padding and surface embroidery can again be incorporated into the design. Straight rows of cable stitch worked in coton à broder on cream polyester/cotton were padded with wadding and applied to a backing fabric to create the main band of the shell (*115*). Random rows of diagonal outline stitch created the movement in the upper band whilst areas of chain stitch, speckling, and padded and manipulated fabrics were used to complete the design.

Whilst every effort should be made to design and plan a project in advance there are times when this is not possible and the

114 *Padding and surface smocking give depth and contrast to the shell panel.* (JEAN HODGES. PHOTO: ANDREW HODGES)

115 *Detail of smocking on the shell panel.* (JEAN HODGES)

116 *Random smocked organza has been manipulated to form a fantasy three-dimensional octopus. The background seashells also make an ideal design source.* (TONI GARDNER)

whole idea simply grows and develops as work proceeds. This is especially true when handling and manipulating fabrics to see how they react under varying conditions. What starts out as a simple experiment with no particular aim can often turn out to be a work of major importance. Just such an occasion arose when a piece of jersey panne velvet was honeycomb-smocked on the back. The result was so luxurious, with the light reflecting off the ripples, that it was essential to enhance and extend this effect. After a great deal of thought it was decided that it would be best to incorporate the strips of smocking with equally luxurious fabrics and trimmings. Antique fabrics, tambour beadwork on silk velvet, lace appliqué, beads, braids and surface stitchery were all incorporated by means of appliqué into the waistcoat which then took on a beautifully rich mediaeval look. This look was helped by the choice of a very simple garment shape giving complete freedom of expression uncluttered by seams and shapings.

When combining smocking and appliqué to create a garment in this manner it is important, as already stated, to choose a very simple style. A waistcoat or jacket with seams only at the shoulders is ideal although other articles could be equally as effective.

Having smocked a piece, or pieces, of fabric in whatever size, weight, texture or colour is

99

117 *Waistcoat in progress. Rich panne velvet, reverse honeycomb-smocked, combines with antique fabrics and laces by means of hand appliqué.* (PAT SALES)

of particular interest, gather together all the materials which could possibly be used in the jacket. Cut the pattern out in a fine calico which will be used as a backing for the appliqué and lay this on a surface where, if possible, it will not need to be disturbed. Place the smocked fabrics onto the calico and 'play' with them by draping, bending, and moulding with the tubes going in different directions, to see the various effects. Surround the smocking with a variety of other materials, discarding any found to be unsuitable. Gradually move and replace pieces until the effect is pleasing and works as a complete design. This may well take some time to accomplish, which is why the article needs to be left out and viewed as a whole from different directions.

Once a pleasing design has been achieved the pieces can be tidied up, the raw edges turned under and applied to the backing calico by hand or machine, depending on the types of fabric used. Beads, braids, ribbons, lace and surface stitchery can then be added as necessary.

Join the shoulder seams and line with a suitable fabric. The edges can be bound with a bias cut binding to complete an exclusive and creative design.

COMBINING TECHNIQUES

Smocking has a richness and depth which some forms of embroidery may lack. It is for these qualities that it can be combined with other techniques, often as a contrast, so that each will complement and enhance the other.

Quilting is one such technique. The sharply etched and tactile appearance of smocking acts as a foil to the subtle, rounded contours of English quilting. An added bonus is that both forms of embroidery are ideally suited to a wide range of garments and articles. An exciting waistcoat or jacket could be designed using a fine fabric such as silk chiffon or lawn and placing horizontally worked smocking at the hem. This could then be manipulated to give movement and allow the fabric to blend into a main area of English quilting with the possible addition of fabric paint and surface stitchery. This combination of techniques would work extremely well if used for a panel or hanging to translate a country scene, rock formation, icicles or a seashore. The corded effect of Italian quilting could enable the design from a smocked panel to spill over and be carried through into a plain unsmocked area.

A variety of fabrics and textures can be successfully combined by means of patchwork techniques. Plain squares can contrast with the heavy texture of deep triple honeycomb and a thin layer of wadding behind the unsmocked areas will maintain the effect (*119*). Pin tucks and pleats can complement the softer lines of smocking on fine lawn or silk. The panels of smocking are mounted onto a thin backing to retain their shape and small back stitches, catching in each tube, are used to join the seams as machining tends to flatten and distort the gathers.

Squares and rectangles are the easiest shapes to start with but there is no reason why others, such as triangles, diamonds, hexagons or octagons should not be considered. As with squares, the smocking is worked, then cut and stitched onto an accurately cut backing fabric. This technique can be used for luxury cushions or bags and for adding textural interest to the centre of a patchwork quilt or hanging.

118 *Silk chiffon gathered, manipulated and then reverse smocked.* (PAULINE MACKENZIE)

119 *Triple honeycomb smocking on cream satin combines with plain areas of fabric backed with wadding to create a patchwork cushion.* (JEAN HODGES)

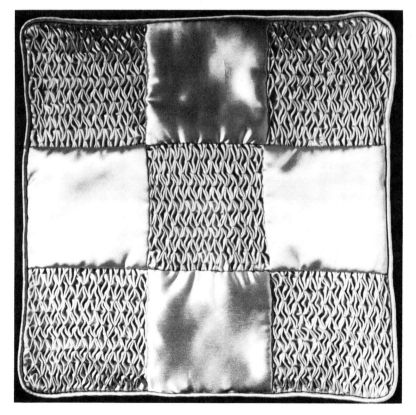

Ten

Experimental Work

All forms of fabric dyeing can be creatively used and are worth considering. Beautiful effects can be achieved by tie-dyeing a smocked piece before removing the gathering threads, whilst space-dyeing and batik are other interesting possibilities.

FABRIC PAINT
Many exciting, imaginative and possibly unexpected effects can be achieved by the use of fabric paints on both traditional and reverse smocking before or after the stitching has been worked. With this in mind the following experiment was carried out. A piece of white satin was gathered at 6 mm ($\frac{1}{2}$ in.) intervals and smocked using triple honey-comb stitch. The sample was stretched slight-ly and tacked to a backing fabric to hold the tubes open. This was then pinned to a vertical surface ready for spraying. The idea was to spray a different colour from each side of the work with the thought that where the two colours met on the surface of the tubes they would blend and form a new colour. This did not, in fact, happen. Standing side on to the smocking (not facing as for normal spray painting) the sample was sprayed pink from one side and blue from the other. The effect was quite fascinating and totally unexpected. Instead of the colours blending, they remain completely separate and, because each colour hits just the side of the tube, it gives the impression of being pearlized when viewed from the front. As the piece is moved the different colours become apparent as though the fabric is 'shot'.

This gave the initial inspiration for the wedding dress and coronet already described on page 69 but is well worth further investiga-tion and development for wider application. The fabric paint was made permanent by leaving in a hot airing cupboard for a day.

Fabric paint was also used to create stripes and add depth to the background of the smocked panels and frilled collar on the smock shown in figure 120. The fabric was prepared by sticking down strips of 6 mm ($\frac{1}{4}$ in.) wide masking tape at 6 mm ($\frac{1}{4}$ in.) intervals to form vertical stripes. The exposed area was painted over with chestnut-coloured fabric paint, the masking tape was then removed and the paint was made permanent with a hot iron. Honeycomb stitch, using a pure linen thread, was worked over the unpainted stripes to bring them forward and then the leaves were applied to complete the design.

By varying the background colours inter-esting scenes could be created which, with added stitchery, could be effectively used in panels and hangings. Transfer paints or crayons could also be used in this manner. Fabric and transfer paints are available in many hardware and craft stores and the crayons can be found in most art shops.

SMOCKING ON KNITTING
The versatility of smocking becomes evident when it is combined with hand or machine knitting. Interesting effects can be achieved by treating simple ribbing as though it was gathered fabric. Not only can smocking be used to give a decorative finish to a neckline, hem, cuff or waistline but it can also become a textural focal point and a background for further embellishment with beads or surface stitchery. An otherwise plain and possibly dull garment can come alive by the use of a contrasting colour scheme for the smocking. Likewise, a yarn containing a lurex or similar thread can add a subtle glitter to catch the light.

120 *A reversible smock brought up to date by means of honeycomb smocking over stripes created with fabric paint on the bodice, collar and sleeve top. Appliqué leaves and Dorset wheel buttons complete the design.* (GILL AXTELL)

A wider range of designs may be obtained if the ribbing is worked to a looser tension than normal, but this depends on the individual worker and the effect required. In order to maintain an even embroidery tension, gathering threads are inserted to hold the ribbing in place and then removed on completion of the work. Experimentation will show which stitches are most suitable for use with knitting but cable, honeycomb, surface honeycomb and diamond stitch can be particularly successful.

With the comparative openness and flexibility of a knitted fabric, it is worth considering more unusual types of 'thread' for working the smocking stitches. Narrow ribbons, braids, cords or even leather thonging could prove to be effective and give a distinctive finish. These would be particularly appropriate if the piece was to be incorporated into a panel, hanging or other decorative and creative project.

FURTHER IDEAS FOR EXPERIMENTAL WORK

Subtle changes of colour or tone can be introduced by running coloured threads down the back of the tubes of a fine fabric in regular or random patterns. This shadow effect can be added before or after the

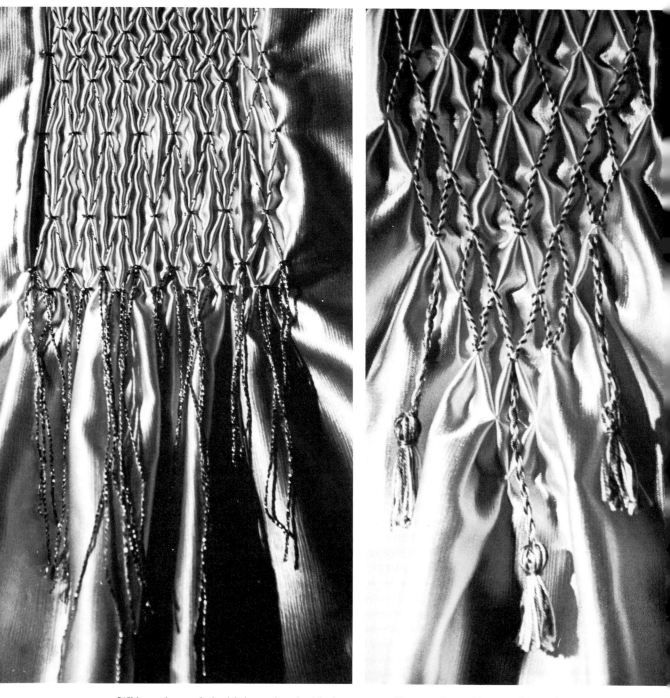

121 *White satin smocked with lurex thread with the ends forming a fringe.* (SUE LACKIE)

122 *Honeycomb smocking on white satin with some tubes given added emphasis by means of surface embroidery in mauve silk. Hand-made tassels complete the design.* (SUE LACKIE)

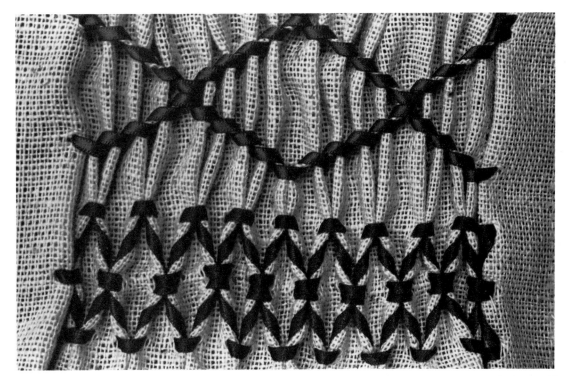

123 *Narrow ribbon worked over a loosely woven fabric.* (SUE LACKIE)

smocking stitches have been worked. Glittery threads or ribbons can be particularly interesting, especially if they are brought to the surface to hang as a fringe or tassels. Tassels can give an extra air of luxury if they are made from a metallic thread or silk and can be added to garments, bags, hangings, lampshades, curtains or luxury cushions.

There are occasions when an added emphasis and richness may be needed and this can be achieved in a number of ways. The tubes can be embroidered before the gathers are pulled up to bring out a specific colour or design; surface embroidery added after the smocking has been worked; or the cells can be filled with beads and stitchery. Beads can also be threaded onto the needle and attached as the tubes are stitched together or they can be threaded so that they hang freely to give sparkle and movement.

With a loosely woven fabric it is possible to use ribbons or braids to work the stitchery. If the tubes run horizontally the ribbons can then be knotted and tied to form a lacy over-pattern (*124*). Narrow ribbons can also be threaded through the smocking stitches (*125*) but care should be taken when securing the ends to ensure that this is done with the smocking stretched to avoid the ribbons pulling when the work is used.

A wide range of pattern and textural effects can be created by working honeycomb smocking over narrow tucks. As the fabric is already held by stitchery the embroidery is purely decorative and gives the opportunity for further development.

SMOCKING VARIATIONS
No chapter on the modern experimental approach to smocking would be complete without some mention of the various other forms which have evolved.

Whilst the gathering threads are being tacked from dot to dot it will be noticed that the fabric undulates to give a subtle furrowed

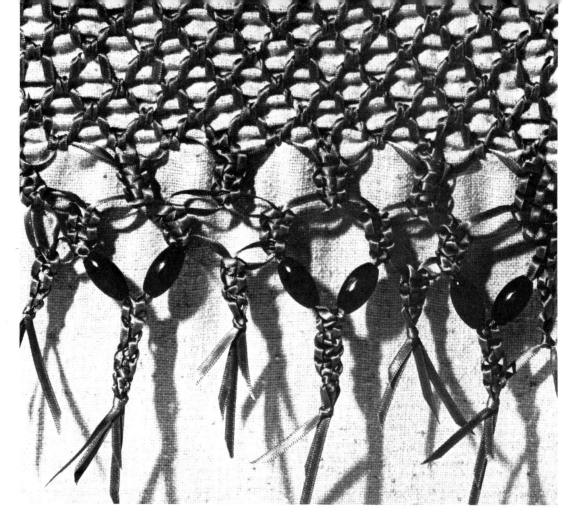

124 *Horizontal smocking using narrow ribbons with the ends knotted and tied in a lacy over-pattern. Beads give added movement.* (CAROLE TOMPKINS)

125 *Narrow ribbon threaded through surface honeycomb stitchery.* (SUE LACKIE)

surface regularly marked by tiny tacks. This furrowed effect can be developed in many ways by running threads through the tacks. It was this observation which inspired the white silk evening bag illustrated in figure 126. Here the rythmic lines were further emphasized and extended by working through a fine layer of wadding sandwiched between a piece of silk and butter muslin. The dots were spaced ~t regular intervals on the muslin side and pickɔd up through all the layers. Soft, spun silk weaving yarn was criss-crossed diagonally through the tacking threads and interspersed with beads. Beads also edge the top of the bag and a fine silk cord with hand-made tassels completes it.

By picking up specified systems of dots,

126 *Silk evening bag. Soft spun silk woven through evenly spaced tacking threads gives a lattice effect.*
(DOROTHY TUCKER. BY KIND PERMISSION OF MARJORIE WILLIAMS)

127 *The construction of the bag in figure 126 ·*

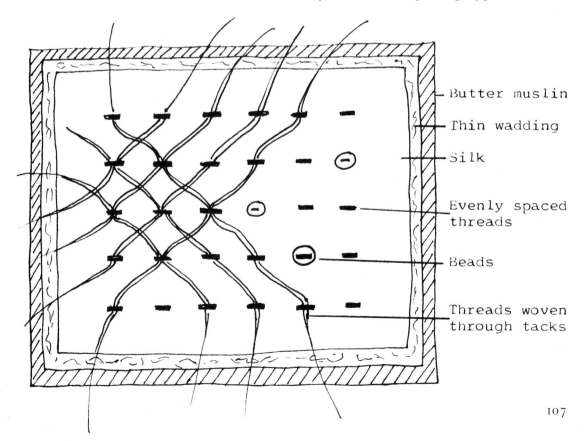

Butter muslin

Thin wadding

Silk

Evenly spaced threads

Beads

Threads woven through tacks

various rich, textural effects can be achieved which are suitable for including in clothing, accessories, furnishings, panels and hangings. No gathering threads are necessary and with only twice the completed amount of fabric being used the work is not elastic. Also, owing to their method of construction these forms of smocking do not have the strength or durability of the traditional work and care should be taken if the article is washed. However, they can prove to be very exciting and well worth investigation.

Lattice or Canadian smocking

Lattice pattern is worked on the wrong side of the fabric and, as the name would suggest, gives a woven, plaited effect. In the past this form was used on cushions and sunhats but has once more found favour in its wider application. It can be inserted into garments or used to create textural interest on collars, cuffs and pockets. Creative embroideries, bed covers and bed valances can also incorporate this technique. Uncrushable materials such as synthetics, velvet, corduroy, satin, fine leather and heavy furnishing fabrics are all suitable and will produce interesting and rich effects.

Mark out a grid of squares with dots placed at 2.5 cm (1 in.) intervals on the back of the fabric. Using a strong thread such as coton à broder, sylko perlé or buttonhole twist make a large knot in the end and work the pattern on the back as follows.

Starting in the top left-hand corner of the grid, pick up dot 1 (*129*) and make a small stitch over it. Pick up dot 2 and then go back to dot 1 and pick this up again. Pull 1 and 2 together and knot securely by making a loop of the thread above the stitches then passing the needle under the stitches and through the loop, taking care not to catch in any fabric. Pick up dot 3. With the thread above the needle, slip the needle under the thread between dots 1/2 and 3 and pull tight to make a knot, keeping the fabric between 1/2 and 3 completely flat. Pick up dot 4, then dot 3, pull together tightly and make a knot. Pick up dot 5 and, with the thread above the needle, slip the needle under the thread between 3/4 and 5 and make a knot, again keeping the fabric flat. Repeat down the row. Work the second row in the same manner and repeat across the area.

Check or gingham fabrics are particularly

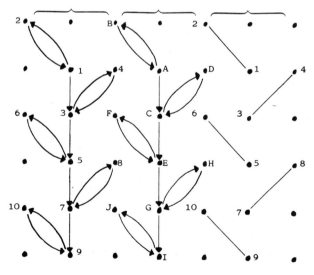

128 *Lattice pattern*

129 *Lattice pattern worked on the cuff of a wool mixture jacket.* (JEAN HODGES)

suitable for this lattice pattern as the squares form a ready-made grid and provide a colour interest.

Flower pattern

Flower pattern gives a highly textural effect and is worked on the right side. Mark a grid with the dots approximately 3 cm $(1\frac{1}{4}$ in.) apart on the front of the fabric. Using a strong thread and working from left to right start at A1 (*131*) and take a small diagonal stitch; do the same at 2, 3 4, and again at 1, slanting the stitches towards the centre. Pull the thread up very tightly and take another small diagonal stitch to secure the fabric. Push the needle through to the wrong side, making sure that it does not catch any of the fabric at the back. Bring the needle out again at B1 and repeat the sequence. Work across the row in this manner and then start the second row and repeat until the area is filled. A bead or French knot can be added in the centre of each flower for extra interest.

Once again, the back of this pattern will be found to be as exciting as the front and offers an opportunity for further development. Ei-

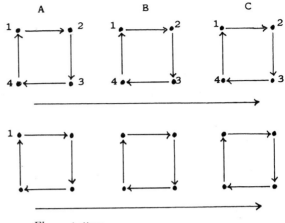

131 *Flower pattern*

ther plain or checked fabric can be explored with the possibility of further colour being added by the use of fabric or transfer paints. If the reverse of the pattern is to be used the grid and all the stitches are worked on the back of the fabric.

All these forms of 'mock' smocking fall naturally into tucks and pleats as against the gathers of the traditional work. The effect can be used to advantage as in the lawn bodice front shown in figure 132 where the textural contrast is enhanced by the addition of hand-made lace.

130 *Flower pattern worked on check taffeta with a bead added at the centre of each flower.* (JEAN HODGES)

132 *Lawn bodice front with added hand-made lace* (LUCINDA GANDERTON)

Eleven

Finishings and Neatenings

As much attention to detail should be given to the finishing and neatening of a hand-made article as to its decoration. Whether the piece of work is complicated or simple in its technique, no amount of ornamentation will correct a poor make-up. Raw edges have to be neatened with the appropriate seam or hem, the corners may need extra care, openings must be fastened, and individual pieces have to be joined together. When the stitchery and decoration have been completed there are often cords, plaits, buttons and beads to be added. All these suggested details require a certain amount of skill, experience and above all, patience. Apart from the basic stitches, seams, hems and turnings well known to anyone interested in embroidery or fashion design, there are the following finishings which may prove helpful:

1 Bias binding
2 Cushion edges
3 Piping
4 Mitred corners
5 Hand-made buttons and loops
6 Plaits and cords

1 BIAS BINDING

The true bias grain of the material runs diagonally across the fabric. Fold the material so that the warp threads lie directly across the weft threads and cut along the fold. Mark lines parallel to this bias edge with tailor's chalk, as far apart from each other as the required width of the binding. Cut along the lines and join the straight edges of the bindings with the right sides together. Stitch the short edges allowing a 6 mm ($\frac{1}{4}$ in.) turning. Trim off the corners and press the join open.

133 *Bias binding*

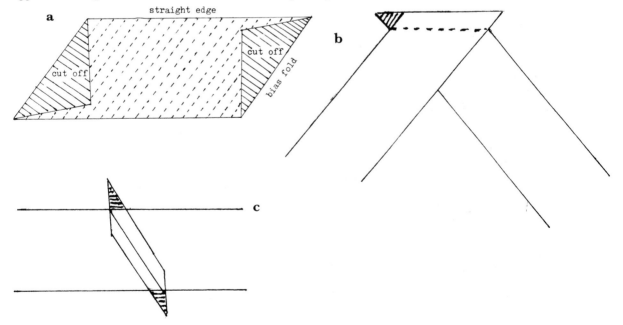

2 CUSHION EDGES

Cushions play an important part in the decorative scheme of the home and they may even form the focal point of interest, so a well-filled well-shaped cushion is essential. The pad helps the finished result but if the front and back edges of the cushion cover are joined along a slightly curved line this eliminates the ugly distortion of the corners.

Measure the pad and allow extra 1.5 cm ($\frac{1}{2}$ in.) turnings all round the two squares of material for the front and back of the cushion; at each corner mark a point with a pin 1.5–2 cm ($\frac{1}{2}$–$\frac{3}{4}$ in.), depending on the size of the cushion, in along the edge of each side. Join the two squares together by a line of tacking from each pin to the centre of the side and to the next pin in a slight curve. Trim off the material leaving a 1.5 cm ($\frac{1}{2}$ in.) turning.

For a plain piping cord cover with strips of bias binding or for ruched piping cut the strips on the straight grain of the fabric; in either case snip the seam allowance at the corners to be sure of a sharp turn of the cord.

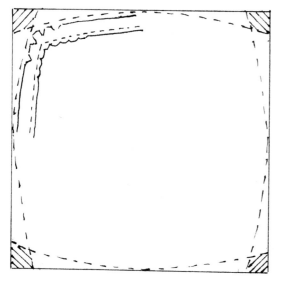

134 *Cushion cover with piping cord inserted, top left. Cut away corners (shaded areas)*

3 PIPING

Piping is made by covering cord with bias-cut fabric which is wide enough to wrap round the cord plus an extra 1.5 cm ($\frac{1}{2}$ in.) either side for turnings.

1 Lay the cord down the centre of the wrong side of the bias-cut strip. Fold the strip in half over the cord. Pin and tack the strip with the wrong sides together and the raw edges matching.

2 Stitch by hand or machine as close to the cord as possible (*135a*).

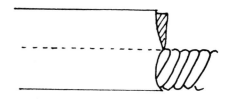

135 *Piping*
a *Fold fabric over piping and stitch*

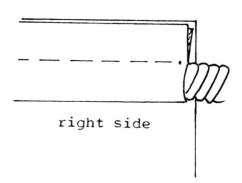

right side

b *Piping placed on right side of first piece of fabric*

3 Place the covered piping on the right side of one edge of the garment or article. Tack in place on the stitching line (*135b*).
4 Place the second piece of fabric wrong side up on top of the piping with all the raw edges lying in one direction.
5 Tack through all the layers on the previous tacking line. Stitch by hand or machine along this line (*135c*). Trim the raw edges to remove unnecessary bulk.

Where a continuous band is necessary the piping should be joined before it is used.

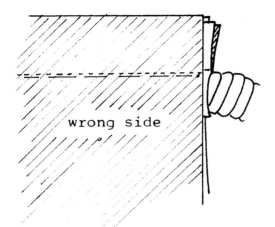

c *Piping sandwiched between fabric and stitched*

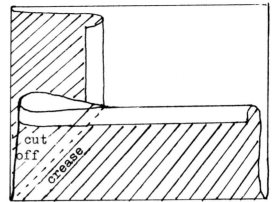

136 *Mitred corner*

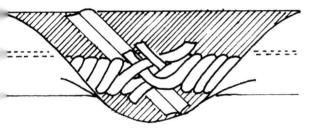

d *Joining lengths of piping*

Measure the length of piping needed and join the bias strips as already described on page 111. Unravel a short length of cord at each end. Trim each of the strands making up the cord to a different length and then twist them round each other as shown (*135d*).

4 MITRED CORNERS

Turn the required width of hem plus 6 mm ($\frac{1}{4}$ in.) up onto the right side of the fabric either side of the corner; turn the raw edges 6 mm ($\frac{1}{4}$ in.) down onto the hem. Even out the corner pleat so as to crease a diagonal line, running from the corner to the matching junction of the two hems; stitch along the creased line and cut off the pleat leaving a 6 mm ($\frac{1}{4}$ in.) turning. Turn the completed corner back onto the wrong side of the fabric. The folds of the hem either side of the corner are now in the correct position to hem down onto the wrong side of the fabric with only the smallest stitch possible appearing on the right side.

5 HAND-MADE BUTTONS AND LOOPS

Hand-made buttons can give a charming and exclusive finish to any garment and ensure a correct match either to the fabric or to the embroidery used.

Ball buttons (*137*)

Use lengths of rouleau or thin cord to make the buttons, keeping them in proportion for the garment: the thinner the cord, the smaller the button will be. Allow about 15–25 cm (6–10 in.) of cord, depending on the thickness, for each button to be made. Following the diagrams and direction arrows carefully, form the button loosely, then gently ease the knot into a ball, making sure the cord loops in the direction indicated. A short shank can be made by stitching the two ends of cord together and tightly wrapping with a matching thread.

Dorset crosswheel buttons (*138*)

Using a thread of suitable thickness according to the size of button to be made, buttonhole stitch all round a plastic curtain ring, pushing the stitches tightly together (casting). Turn the buttonholing so that the ridge of the stitches is inside the ring (slicking). Secure a new long thread with a firm back stitch at the back and wrap around the ring, moving the

113

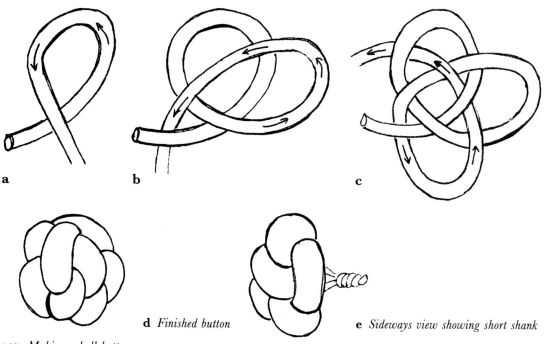

a **b** **c**

d *Finished button* **e** *Sideways view showing short shank*

137 *Making a ball button*

138 *Dorset wheel button*

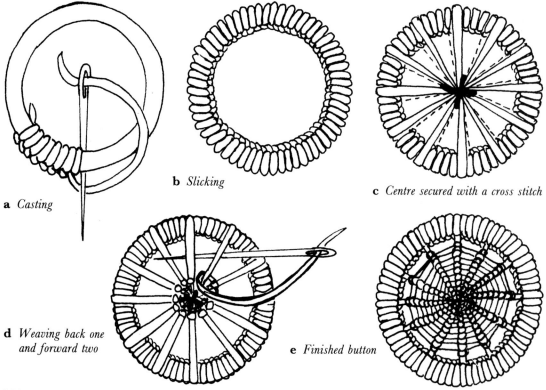

a *Casting* **b** *Slicking* **c** *Centre secured with a cross stitch*

d *Weaving back one and forward two* **e** *Finished button* thread a little at each turn until there are between eight and 12 spokes depending on the size of button being made. Bring the needle up in the middle and secure the front and back spokes with a firm cross stitch where they overlap. Work a spider's web from the centre outwards by back stitching over one spoke and moving forward two. Variations in colour and weight of thread can give a very attractive effect.

Fabric loops

Fabric loops are a decorative form of fastening made from a rouleau strip and are generally used with ball buttons. They can be used singly at the top of a slit opening, spaced on an overlapping opening or close together as a special feature. Ideally, the loops are inserted into a seam but if this is not possible they can be stitched by hand to a garment edge, although this is not a very strong method.

To insert accurately a row of loops into a seam it helps if the rouleau is tacked to a piece of paper which has been marked out into equal sections. Carefully arrange the rouleau over these marks and tack straight down each edge of the paper. Position the paper on the outside of the garment with the part of the loop intended to go over the button facing away from the edge. Tack and then machine or back stitch through the loops, paper and garment, making sure the stitching is on the seam line of the garment. Remove the tacking and gently tear away the paper. Place the

139 *Rows of loops tacked on to paper and stitched in place*

140 *Spaced loops stitched in place*

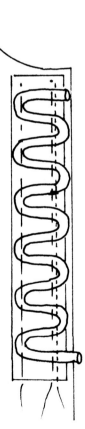

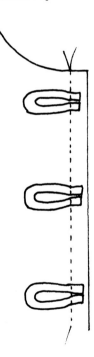

garment facing right side down onto the loops. Tack and stitch on exactly the same seam line. Trim away any excess fabric but not the loops.

If single or spaced loops are to be used, cut lengths of rouleau and carefully mark each one with the amount needed to go over the button. Place the loops in position on the outside of the garment with the marks running through the seam line and the loops facing away from the edge. Machine or back stitch in place and finish with a facing.

Thread loops
Thread loops can be used where buttonholes or rouleau loops would be unsuitable. This is not a strong fastening but can be useful for edge-to-edge openings such as on baby clothes, nightdresses or neck openings.

Use a double thread, lightly waxed to avoid separation, and knot the end. Take a small back stitch through the edge of the garment to secure the thread. Make a stitch equal in length to the diameter of the button, sliding the needle through the edge of the fabric to emerge by the knot and so form a long back stitch. Make three more of these stitches in the same place, checking as each thread is added that the button will pass through easily. Work close buttonhole stitch over the threads to complete the loop and fasten off by taking two or three stitches into the edge of the fabric.

141 *Thread loops*

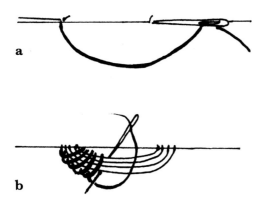

a

b

6 PLAITS AND CORDS

Plaits can take the place of piping cords to neaten the edges of cushions, boxes and bags. The size of the plait depends on the thickness of the threads and the number of ends used to make up the plait. The black and white cushion shown in figure 36, page 27, has a plait made-up from five ends of four-ply wool, two ends white and three ends black.

The yoke of the folk-dancing blouse (colour plate 3) is tied at the neck with a pair of twisted cords. Measure two lengths of thread rather longer than twice the finished length required, tie the two ends together and stretch them out taut, between two hooks. Insert a pencil or stick in between the threads and rotate it until the twisted cord takes up the full length. Remove from the hooks and fold the cord in half, then allow it to re-twist itself freely to make the final cord; the ends can be bound round and made into a tassel.

142 *Plait*

Suppliers

UK

H.F. Lock and Son
Swan Lane
Guildford
Surrey
Good quality fabrics

Geoffrey Magnay Ltd
Boulters Barn
Chipping Norton
Oxfordshire
Gathering machines and accessories

Needle and Thread
80 High Street
Horsell
Woking
Surrey
Embroidery threads and books

Threadneedle House
9 Nuneham Courtenay
Oxford
Embroidery requisites and threads

USA

Adventures in Crafts
218 East 81 Street
New York
NY 100028

American Handicrafts
Box 9680
Fort Worth
TX 76107

Commonwealth Felt Co.
211 Congress Street
Boston
MA 02110

Newark Dressmaker Supply Co.
4616 Park Drive
Bath
PA 18014

Hazel Pearson Handicrafts
16017 E Valley Blvd
City of Industry
CA 91744

Lee Wards
1200 St Charles Street
Elgin
IL 60120

Erica Wilson Needle Works
717 Madison Av
New York
NY 10021

Smocking Groups and Societies

UK
Smocking Group of the Embroiderers'
Guild
Apartment 41
Hampton Court Palace
East Molesey
Surrey KT8 9AU
Tel: 01 943 1229

USA
Smocking Arts Guild of America
P.O. Box 75
Knoxville
TN 37901

Book List

BROWN, Pauline, *Embroidery Backgrounds: Painting and Dyeing Techniques*, Batsford 1984

VINCENTE-DEAN, Audrey, *Smocking: A Practical Beginners' Guide*, Stanley Paul

DESIGNERS' GUILD, *Soft Furnishings: Ideas and Fabrics*, Pan 1980

FISHBURN, Angela, *The Batsford Book of Lampshades*, Batsford 1984

HOWARD, Constance, *Embroidery and Colour*, Batsford 1976

LEE, Pamela, and HAWKSLEY, Rozanne, *Pattern Designing and Adaptation for Beginners*, Granada 1981

HODGES, Jean, *Smocking Design*, Batsford 1987

HOWARD, Constance, *The Constance Howard Book of Stitches*, Batsford 1979